★ OLD-SCHOOL WOODSHOP ACCESSORIES ★

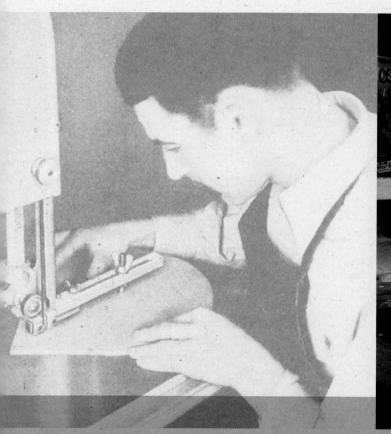

CHRIS GLEASON

POPULAR WOODWORKING BOOKS
CINCINNATI, OHIO
www.popularwoodworking.com

READ THIS IMPORTANT SAFETY NOTICE

METRIC CONVERSION CHART

to convert	to	multiply by
Inches	Centimeters	2.54
Centimeters	Inches	0.39
Feet	Centimeters	30.5
Centimeters	Feet	0.03
Yards	Meters	0.91
Meters	Yards	1.09

OLD-SCHOOL WOODSHOP ACCESSORIES. Copyright © 2007 by Chris Gleason. Printed and bound in China. All rights reserved. No part of this book may be reproduced in any form or by any electronic or mechanical means including information storage and retrieval systems without permission in writing from the publisher, except by a reviewer, who may quote brief passages in a review. Published by Popular Woodworking Books, an imprint of F+W Publications, Inc., 4700 East Galbraith Road, Cincinnati, Ohio, 45236. First edition.

Distributed in Canada by Fraser Direct
100 Armstrong Avenue
Georgetown, Ontario L7G 5S4
Canada

Distributed in the U.K. and Europe by David & Charles
Brunel House
Newton Abbot
Devon TQ12 4PU
England
Tel: (+44) 1626 323200
Fax: (+44) 1626 323319
E-mail: postmaster@davidandcharles.co.uk

Distributed in Australia by Capricorn Link
P.O. Box 704
Windsor, NSW 2756
Australia

Visit our Web site at www.popularwoodworking.com for information on more resources for woodworkers.

Other fine Popular Woodworking Books are available from your local bookstore or direct from the publisher.

11 10 09 08 07   5 4 3 2 1

Library of Congress Cataloging-in-Publication Data

Gleason, Chris
    Old-school woodshop accessories / by Chris Gleason. -- 1st ed.
        p. cm.
    Includes index.
    ISBN-13: 978-1-55870-808-2 (pbk. : alk. paper)
    ISBN-10: 1-55870-808-1 (pbk. : alk. paper)
    1. Woodworking tools. I. Title.
    TT186.G54 2007
    684'.08--dc22

                                        2006039347

ACQUISITIONS EDITOR: David Thiel
SENIOR EDITOR: Jim Stack
DESIGNER: Brian Roeth
PRODUCTION COORDINATOR: Jennifer Wagner
PHOTOGRAPHER: Chris Gleason
PROJECT OPENERS PHOTOGRAPHER: Richer Images
ILLUSTRATOR: Kevin Pierce

ABOUT THE AUTHOR

Chris Gleason has owned and operated Gleason Woodworking Studio for nearly a decade. A self-taught craftsman, he specializes in contemporary furniture and cabinetry. He is particularly inspired by mid-century Danish modern designs.

With a degree in French from Vassar College, in Poughkeepsie, New York, Chris had the opportunity to live and study abroad for a year in Switzerland. The mountain influence must've grabbed hold, as he now makes his home in Salt Lake City, Utah where he bikes and skis as much as possible. He is also an enthusiastic old-time banjo and fiddle player.

ACKNOWLEDGEMENTS

Writing this book gave me the opportunity to look back and consider the history of the craft that I practice every day. It was great to see that the original Deltagrams presented so many clever ideas that are just as relevant today as they were sixty and seventy years ago.

I am thankful to Jim Stack at F+W Publications for approaching me with this project and for his continual help in bringing it to completion.

I had first admired Kevin Pierce's phenomenal illustrations in a book a couple of years ago and I was thrilled when I learned that he would be involved with this project. I owe him a huge thank you. In addition to providing useful information, his drawings contribute to the tone and feel of this book as a whole.

I would also like to thank my wife Michele for all of her patience and support.

TABLE OF CONTENTS

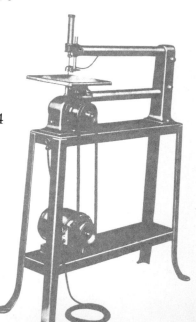

introduction

★ ★

BEFORE the concept for this book came my way I had never seen any of the once-popular Deltagrams. As I perused them for the first time, I wasn't sure which I liked more: the striking style—the graphic design or the clever problem-solving behind the jigs and fixtures. It is clear these vintage publications have a lot to offer for connoisseurs of both aesthetics and functionality.

My goal for this book was to take an earnest look at the ideas presented in some of these old Deltagrams and present their content to a modern audience. Nearly all of the concepts are just as useful today as they were sixty years ago, but some updates have made them a bit more suited to today's woodworking shops. The Drill Bit Caddy in chapter sixteen has had a complete face lift, due largely to the fact that drill bits are now sold with reasonably effective plastic organizers—apparently this wasn't always the case. A few of the techniques seemed a little dangerous, so I re-interpreted those ideas to retain the spirit of the originals while substantially reducing their inherent riskiness. A good example of this is the simple addition of a sturdy handle in chapter three. Most of the projects, though, have been re-created almost exactly from the originals. As a bonus, I have created four chapters which focus on improved workshop storage.

I hope you enjoy these Deltagrams as much as I have. I think they provide a colorful look back at early 20th-century woodworking. And, maybe it is just me, but they seem to point to something I've suspected for a while—some techniques and tools may change over time, but thoughtful problem-solving never goes out of style.

—*Chris Gleason, Salt Lake City, Utah*

SHOP KINKS WORTH KNOWING

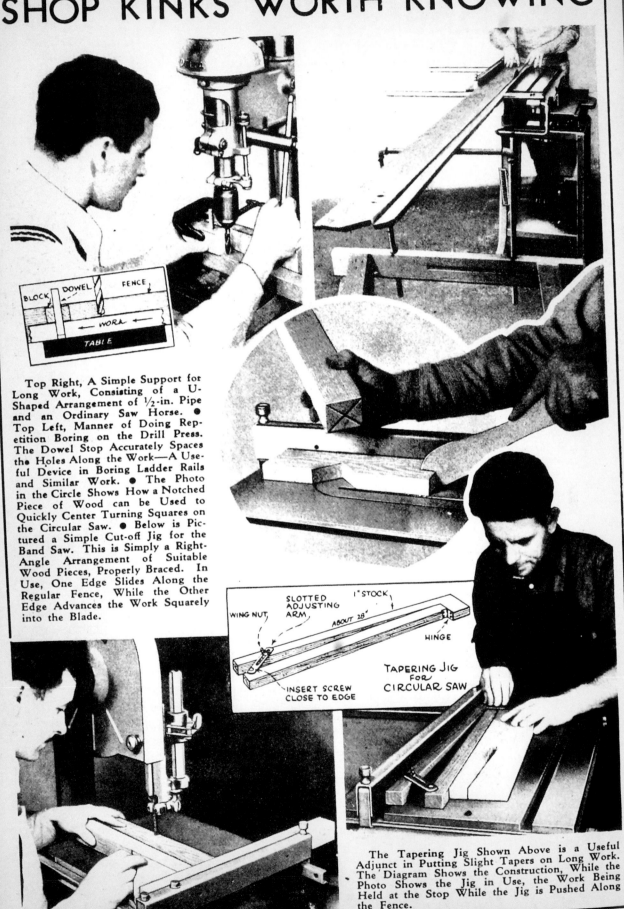

Top Right, A Simple Support for Long Work, Consisting of a U-Shaped Arrangement of ½-in. Pipe and an Ordinary Saw Horse. ● Top Left, Manner of Doing Repetition Boring on the Drill Press. The Dowel Stop Accurately Spaces the Holes Along the Work—A Useful Device in Boring Ladder Rails and Similar Work. ● The Photo in the Circle Shows How a Notched Piece of Wood can be Used to Quickly Center Turning Squares on the Circular Saw. ● Below is Pictured a Simple Cut-off Jig for the Band Saw. This is Simply a Right-Angle Arrangement of Suitable Wood Pieces, Properly Braced. In Use, One Edge Slides Along the Regular Fence, While the Other Edge Advances the Work Squarely into the Blade.

The Tapering Jig Shown Above is a Useful Adjunct in Putting Slight Tapers on Long Work. The Diagram Shows the Construction, While the Photo Shows the Jig in Use, the Work Being Held at the Stop While the Jig is Pushed Along the Fence.

A VERY BRIEF HISTORY OF THE DELTAGRAM

IT WAS the early 1930s and the founder of the Delta Manufacturing Co., Herbert E. Tautz, was enjoying successful sales of his woodworking machines, but he thought the company could do better. In looking at the home woodworking market he theorized the problem was a shortage of printed information promoting and demonstrating woodworking machinery.

To educate the public, Tautz established Delta's Woodworker's Educational Department. Out of it would come 40 years of well-written, profusely illustrated manuals and the birth of the first woodworking magazine: *The Deltagram*. The first issue of *The Deltagram* was published in January of 1932 and the 9" × 6" magazine contained 16 glossy pages with black and white illustrations. You couldn't subscribe or buy an issue on the newsstand. Delta mailed the magazine free to everyone who purchased a Delta machine.

At first *The Deltagram* was published bimonthly and only during the winter months. These were the peak months for building for many home woodworkers. In December 1933, editors unveiled the first color cover with a hand-tinted illustration of a craftsman putting the finishing touches on a toy soldier.

Over the next five years *The Deltagram* enjoyed great success reaching a readership of 75,000 Delta machine owners and—and it was still free! Delta executives toyed with the idea of asking for a nominal subscription, but ultimately rejected the concept in favor of offering individual copies (starting in January, 1938) for ten-cents each. Altruism gave way to business acumen in October 1939, when it was announced that *The Deltagram* would be sold by subscription only, for the price of fifty cents a year.

The Deltagram continued to be published during World War II, with frequent appeals to support the war effort, including suggesting that readers hold off buying new woodworking machinery in lieu of war bonds. Projects in the magazine included flag cases and toy machine guns, tanks and rifles for the kids. Everyone was fully behind the war effort.

With the September 1943 issue, a number of changes affected *The Deltagram*. The publication went to a monthly subscription schedule, and after holding prices static for ten years, the subscription rate went to seventy-five cents a year, or fifteen cents a copy.

The Deltagram continued to publish with changes occurring every few years to keep things current. The magazine changed to an 8" × 11" format in February, 1950, and in August 1950 the editors announced they would begin accepting projects and articles from their readers for publication. The title would change slightly (reflecting changing ownership), and prices would increase to keep up with inflation.

Finally, after weathering the Great Depression and a World War, *The Deltagram* succumbed to progress. The final issue (still only 30 cents an issue) was published in December 1972. It may be no surprise that only three years later the inaugural issue of *Fine Woodworking* magazine would be published, followed by a number of how-to woodworking magazines that all owe some bit of their heritage to *The Deltagram*. We hope this book serves as an appropriate homage to those early editors who were forward-thinking enough to recognize the benefit of educating the home woodworker.

— *The Editors*

A Simple CLOCK CASE

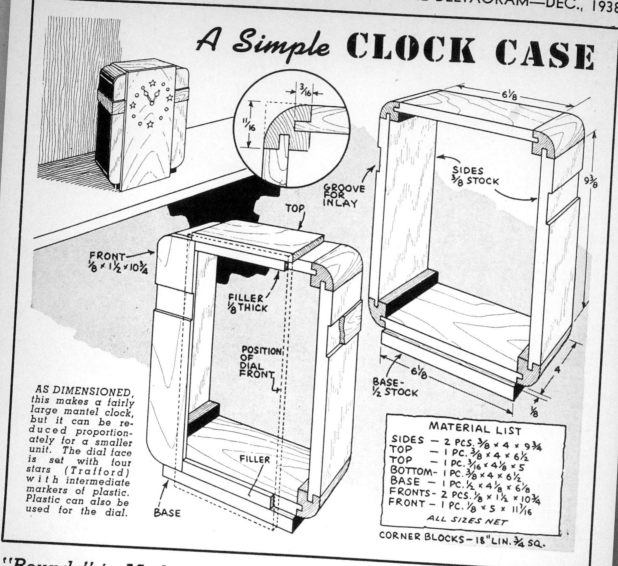

GROOVE FOR INLAY

TOP

FRONT
⅛ × 1½ × 10¾

FILLER ⅛ THICK

POSITION OF DIAL FRONT

FILLER

BASE

SIDES ⅜ STOCK

6⅛

9⅜

BASE— ½ STOCK

6⅛

4

⅛

AS DIMENSIONED, this makes a fairly large mantel clock, but it can be reduced proportionately for a smaller unit. The dial face is set with four stars (Trafford) with intermediate markers of plastic. Plastic can also be used for the dial.

MATERIAL LIST	
SIDES	— 2 PCS. ⅜ × 4 × 9¾
TOP	— 1 PC. ⅜ × 4 × 6½
TOP	— 1 PC. 3/16 × 4⅛ × 5
BOTTOM	— 1 PC. ⅜ × 4 × 6½
BASE	— 1 PC. ½ × 4⅛ × 6⅛
FRONTS	— 2 PCS. ⅛ × 1½ × 10¾
FRONT	— 1 PC. ⅛ × 5 × 11 11/16

ALL SIZES NET

CORNER BLOCKS — 18" LIN. ¾ SQ.

"Rounds" in Modern Furniture Construction

cut does not produce a perfect round. In most cases, however, it is a comparatively simple job to finish the inner curve to a perfect round by sanding, using either hand or machine equipment. The best type of joint is mortise-tenon. A choice of methods is offered here since the mortise can be either routed on the drill press, dadoed on the circular saw or cut on the shaper. The shaper is undoubtedly the best tool since both mortise and tenon can be cut to a perfect match.

Similar methods are used in the construction of the three-way joint with rounded corners, a typical corner being made up as shown in Fig. 4 on the preceding page.

———

ON THE COVER. The cover picture for this issue pictures a machine operation in the shop of the Commercial Woodwork Co., Milwaukee. The job is the cutting of coat hangers used in modern luggage. The company produces over 125,000 of these annually.

"Wood" You Believe It?

THE ENGLISH HAVE A WORD FOR IT! THIS IS CRAMPING

CLAMP-CRAMP RABBET-REBATE

... and this is a REBATE

1

SPIRAL TURNING ON THE TABLE SAW

If you enjoy making period furniture reproductions, or if you've got a repair project on your hands, the ability to turn spirals easily without a lathe might be appealing. And even if you're not in either of these situations, you might find yourself looking around for opportunities to put this fixture to work.

A variety of patterns and sizes can be created by simply varying the miter gauge angles. This technique will work on round stock of any diameter.

Because this process involves operating the table saw in an unusual manner, I suggest working slowly and carefully. I also suggest that you practice on scrap stock first.

Spiral TURNING on the Circular Saw

SPIRAL turnings, ordinarily produced by a slow lathe method, can be greatly simplified by the machine method of making them on the circular saw. Figs. 1 and 2 show the first operation. An auxiliary fence is screw-fastened to the miter gage, after which the fence is clamped to the saw table, as shown in Fig. 2. The blade is exposed to a depth of 3/16 in., and the center of the blade should be in line with the center of the work. The work, when pushed along the fence, will both turn and feed itself, cutting a perfect spiral groove which will not vary over 1/32 in. from any one spiral to the next in line. A fairly stiff blade is necessary, such as the hollow-ground saw or a single dado cutter.

After cutting the spiral groove, the fence is swung completely around to a position about 60° on the opposite side, as can be seen in Fig. 3. The fence is fitted with a guide pin, as shown in the phantom view, Fig. 3, the pin being located so that, engaged in the spiral groove, the bottom of the groove will be immediately over the style B moulding cutter, which is used for the second operation. With the pin guiding the work, the stock is fed to the cutter. The cut produced is not the true shape of the cutter, but is a perfect cove cut, as can be seen in Fig. 4. The cut will be quite smooth if the work is fed slowly, and, of course, it will be just as perfect as the guiding spiral groove.

The work is now mounted in the lathe and the sharp corners of the cove-cut spiral are rounded over.

Perfect Spirals on Round Stock are Easily Cut with the Circular Saw Method.

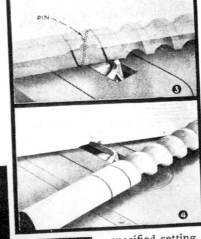

This part of the work is done with a rasp file in the usual manner of making spiral turnings. Finishing can be done with sandpaper held around a dowel stick, as shown in Fig. 5, chasing up the spiral as the work rotates at slow speed. It can be seen that by grinding special cutters, the full round of the spiral can be cut instead of the cove shape. On the average home workshop job, however, this extra labor is not worth while. On the other hand, any job calling for four spiral turnings can be speeded up considerably by using the style B knife in the manner described. The stock shown in the pictures is about 1½ in. diameter, but any other size can be worked equally well. The specified setting of the miter gage in cutting the guiding spiral will give a pleasing pitch, but can be varied to suit. In every case, the spiral-turned portion should be worked first, after which the work can be placed in the lathe for regular turning operations.

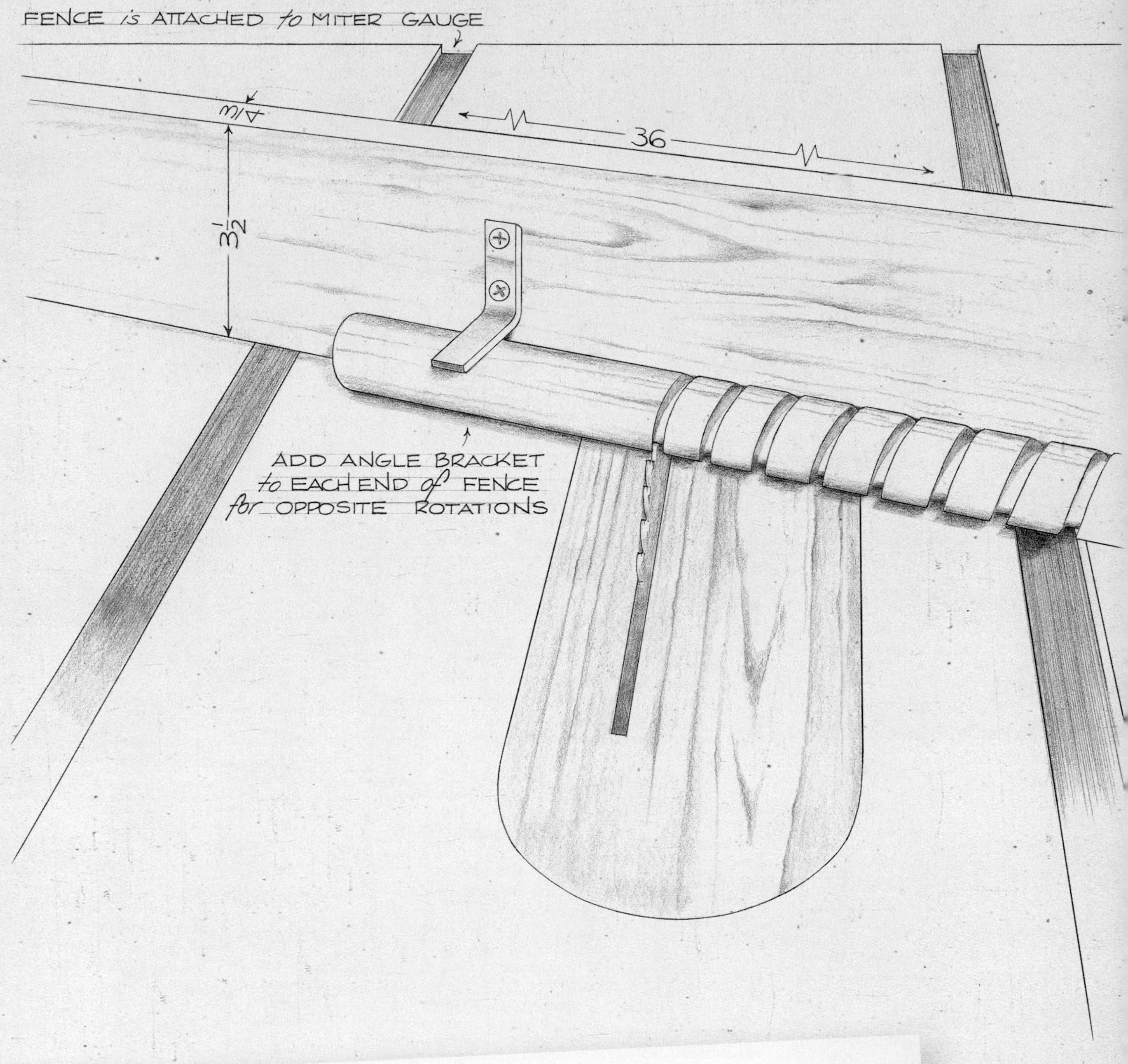

FENCE *is* ATTACHED *to* MITER GAUGE

36

$3\frac{1}{2}$

$\frac{3}{4}$

ADD ANGLE BRACKET
to EACH END *of* FENCE
for OPPOSITE ROTATIONS

parts list

| NO. | COMPONENT | MATERIAL | THICKNESS X WIDTH X LENGTH | |
			INCHES	MILLIMETERS
1	fence extension	1×4	$\frac{3}{4} \times 3\frac{1}{2} \times 36$	19 × 89 × 914
1	L-bracket	metal	$1\frac{1}{2}$	38

❶ The process begins by attaching a 48"-long auxiliary fence to your miter gauge. With the miter gauge positioned at 73°, clamp it down to the table saw top. This will leave both of your hands free to guide the stock and it will help create a cleaner and more even cut. You can determine the correct front-to-back position of the miter gauge by raising the blade to $^3/_{16}$" and setting the dowel in place. As a rule of thumb, the highest point of the blade should be at or near the center of the dowel.

❷ With the dowel still in place, attach a metal angle bracket to the fence so that it is snug against the dowel but not so tight that you can't move the dowel. This will make it much easier to control the dowel as you feed it across the blade. Before I added this bracket as a hold-down I had a difficult time using this fixture.

❸ To advance the dowel, start with your fingers at the bottom of the dowel and rotate them up and towards you. If you walk to the right side of the table saw and look at the end of the dowel, this would be a counter-clockwise rotation. The dowel will be surprisingly easy to rotate, and the spirals will naturally be perfectly aligned—I haven't seen more than $^1/_{32}$" of variation. Add an extra 6" or 8" to the end of each length of dowel that you'll be planning to turn—you'll need a place for your fingers to rotate the dowel. This extra length will be cut off once the turning is done.

❹ At this point, your next step depends on the final result that you're after. I recommend experimenting a bit. In this example, I removed the miter gauge and fence and swung them to 60° on the opposite side. During this step, it is necessary to attach a small pin to the back of the fence; this pin will ride in the groove that was cut on the initial pass. The pin should be located in such a way that the bottom of the groove is directly above the blade. A small discrepancy in the location of this pin will make it difficult to advance the dowel, so if you're having problems, try moving the pin. (The pin is circled in red in the photo.)

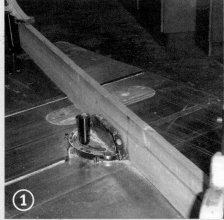

❺ To feed the dowel, work on the left side of the fence and use a metal angle bracket to control the dowel. The rotation direction is the opposite of that used during the initial pass. For me, this is easiest if I stand in front of the table saw—pretty counterintuitive, but it works. To make some of the profiles shown here and many more, adjust the angle of the miter gauge. I used a 73° angle for the initial pass, but I varied the angle from 60° to 73° on the second pass—it makes a big difference.

❻ Once you're happy with the spiral, clean up any milling marks using a drill press equipped with a sanding drum. This should only take a few minutes. I recommend using 80- and 150-grit sandpaper. Finish sanding is easy to do using a sanding pad with 150-grit sandpaper.

TABLE SAW CUTOFF FENCE

2

If you need to cross-cut a large quantity of pieces to the same length, measuring and marking each piece usually becomes tedious and inefficient. This fixture provides a way to cross-cut on the table saw with no measuring required. It will save a lot of time, and it provides consistent results. If you prefer, the fence can also be attached to a miter saw.

Drill the holes at whatever intervals you like—I drilled ¼"-diameter holes spaced 1" apart on center. You can simply mark out a row of holes with a ruler, or you could use a scrap of pegboard as a template.

SHOP HINTS

CUT OFF FENCE

By fastening a board ¾ x 3 x 24 inches to the miter gage and drilling ¼ inch holes spaced 1 inch apart to take a ¼ inch dowel makes an easy way to cut up short lengths of stock to length without use of a rule. Lines are scribed with figures above the holes as shown in pl.oto below.

MAKING DOWELS

When short pieces of dowels are needed the jig made of ½ x 1 ⅝ x 5" cold rolled steel with ¾, ½, ⅜ and ¼ holes as shown above will work out very well. To make clean dowels, bore the holes a trifle smaller and then ream out to size.

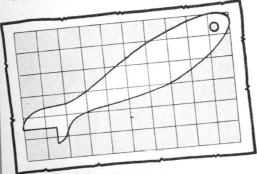

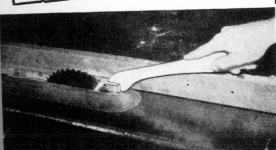

PUSH STICKS

Very often narrow pieces of stock are ripped on the circular saw. The push stick in the photo is very handy. The push stick shown in the upper photo is very useful for planing thin boards on the jointer. The handle is the same as those used on hand planes.

parts list

NO.	COMPONENT	MATERIAL	THICKNESS X WIDTH X LENGTH	
			INCHES	**MILLIMETERS**
1	fence extension	1×4	$^3/_4 \times 2^1/_2 \times 30$	$19 \times 64 \times 762$
1	dowel	birch	$^3/_{16}$ D $\times 1^1/_2$	5 D $\times$ 38

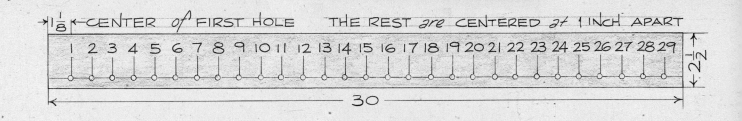

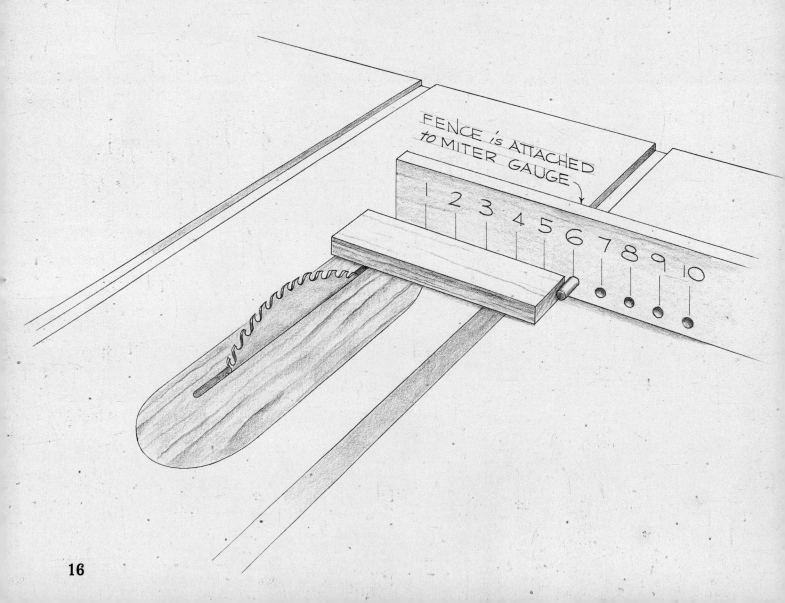

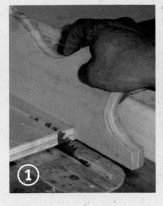

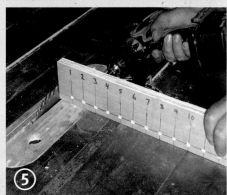

❶ To make the fence, I cut a $3/4" \times 2^1/2" \times 30"$ strip of scrap plywood.

❷ The center of the first hole should be $1^1/8"$ from the left side of the fence and all subsequent holes should be spaced at 1" centers. I used a ruler to mark out these locations and a speed square to extend the marks into a row of long, highly visible lines.

❸ Use a straightedge to draw a line from end to end on the fence. I set the line $1/2"$ up from the bottom edge of the fence.

❹ Drill holes at the intersections of the vertical and horizontal lines. Use a drill press or a handheld drill. Use a brad-point bit to precisely locate the drill on the marks. After the holes are drilled, I used a dark marker to label the holes for quick reference.

❺ I placed the end of the fence against the blade and screwed the fence to the miter gauge using two $1^1/2"$ screws.

❻ To use the gauge, insert a dowel in the appropriate hole. To be safe when cutting, push the miter gauge all the way past the blade, then remove the piece of stock that is on the fixture. The offcut will safely slide away to the right of the blade.

❼ To set up the fixture on the miter saw, pull the blade down and position the fixture up against the blade just as you would on the table saw. Secure the fixture in this spot and make sure to attach a spacer of equal thickness on the left side of the blade.

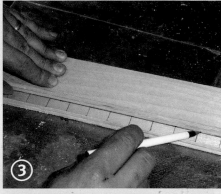

The Deltagram

The Deltagram

Published for Owners of Delta Shops Everywhere

JAMES TATE—Editor

Vol. I

MAY, 1932

No. 3

"Without tools man is nothing; with tools he is all."—CARLYLE

Beating the Depression

RAYMOND DUNCAN, brother of the late Isadora, once said that "every man has been given wits and a pair of hands to work with, and he doesn't need to depend on any other man for his bread . . . This conviction that we must depend on someone else is a curse: it deadens our initiative, our latent faculties. If we lose a job we sit down, fold our hands and wait until someone gives us another job. The thing to do is to break this hypnotic sense, take our hands and our wits and go out and start something useful. The first attempt generally turns out badly, but it leads to something better."

Duncan's projected "cathedral of the arts and crafts" in Paris, the contract for which has recently been signed, is a tribute to his faith in this idea, and a concrete instance of the fact that it works. If all the instances of the efficacy of faith in this idea are not as spectacular as Duncan's $250,000 venture, many of those we run across every day are just as convincing, and just as interesting.

Here is a letter from Ed Hall, of Tell City, Indiana, in which he says: "You will note the letter head we have got out; we have a complete system of sales blanks, etc. All of this business worked up since November 11, 1931. Yes, sir; I consider the war was over since last Armistice Day, when I received my Delta equipment. That I most truly and sincerely mean." Ed's letterhead shows that he does woodcarving, makes wood novelties; makes antique reproductions, wrought-iron work, ship models, and all kinds of interior finish. Now the point here is this: We often hear from someone in a small town, writing to this effect: "I would like to turn my tools to some effect during this depression, in order to offset a salary cut, but there does not seem to be anything to do around this neighbourhood or section:" Tell City is a town of about 4,000 people, down on the Ohio river at the southern end of Indiana. If Ed Hall can make a good living there with the aid of his Delta tools and his native ingenuity there must be opportunities galore in a town of 20,000 to 50,000. And the opportunities are there; the letters we get every day prove it. The case cited above is selected only because Ed's letter happened to come in while we were thinking about this problem.

Or take the case of Bernard J. Roemer, of Colorado Springs, Colo., a story that is familiar to all those who have read our booklet "What Others Have Done with Delta Tools". A bed-fast invalid for more than five years, he has built up a business that is national in scope, with nothing more elaborate in equipment than one of the old Delta Scroll saws, plus a whale of a lot of grit, initiative and tenacity. And is he worried about what is going to happen if the present demand for his jig-saw puzzles peters out? He is not. He is already laying plans, and is determined that his tools will continue to afford him a good living as well as a pleasant occupation.

Or consider L. D. Fluent, of Richmond Hill, N. Y. Sixty-five year old, and with but one hand, he started out "cold" in a strange neighbourhood with nothing but his Delta machinery and his courage. In three months, to use his own words, he has been enabled to "catch up on back rent, pay some debts, make payment when due and make a fair living . . . my prospects are good for building up a nice business for myself."

We could go on for page after page with instances of Delta owners who have beaten the depression, and, incidentally, have lifted themselves beyond all future fear of depressions. You may be one of the fortunate ones who have no need of using your tools to supplement your income. But if you are not, then look around you. Somewhere near there are people who need something in the way of woodwork; it is not the simplest part of the job to connect with these people, but with a little ingenuity it can be done.

"Can a man by taking thought add a cubit to his stature?" asked the prophet. Perhaps not. But you can bet your life that a man by taking thought can add considerably to his income. And as far as adding to his stature is concerned, I'm afraid the prophet would lose if he propounded that query to a chap with a Delta saw, for that ingenious gentlemen would take thought—and then go make himself a pair of stilts.

TABLE SAW JIG FOR
CUTTING WEDGES AND SHORT TAPERS

I occasionally need a handful of wedges in a uniform size and this jig provides a way to make them quickly and consistently. I also build a number of coffee and end tables which feature tapered legs and this jig helps to speed up those projects too. You'll notice the angle and size of the cut can be adjusted by twisting the bolt in or out. The original jig had a rather elaborate adjustment mechanism—I replaced it with a simple T-nut. A 4"-long bolt will provide a good range of adjustment.

I couldn't resist making one other modification to the design. For safety's sake, I attached a handle. I used my band saw to cut out a handle which is similar in shape to those traditionally found on handplanes and attached it to the base plate of the jig. The exact location of the handle isn't critical—I simply wanted to be able to firmly grip the jig with my hand well out of harm's way.

I'd be surprised if this jig wouldn't come in handy in your shop, but if nothing else, you can always develop a line of custom-made solid-wood doorstops from scraps.

The Deltagram

Practical IDEAS for the Craftsman

One of the most important things in using screw fastenings with plugged holes (see the Cobbler's Bench on page 10) is the matter of keeping the countersunk hole perfectly round. Care should be used in drilling that the chuck does not spin out the wood, and some protection against screwdriver slips, such as the simple board shown at the left, should be used.

STEEL STRIP

THIS EDGE SHOULD TOUCH SAW BLADE WHEN BLOCK IS SET OVER TO THE END OF SLOT

SLOT

PIVOT POINT

STOP SHOULDER

¾ x 5½ x 10

The photograph and drawing above show a simple jig for putting fast tapers on tent stakes, pickets and the like. A steel or hardwood strip is made to exactly fit the groove in the saw table, and to this strip is fastened the adjustable wood block. This block pivots on a bolt at the point shown, while a second bolt works in a slot to give the necessary taper. The jig should just clear the saw blade when pushed completely over.

A SET OF THESE SIMPLE JIGS PERMITS RAPID CENTERING OF STOCK TURNINGS

When beveling large pieces of wood or frames on the jointer, you will find it much easier to get a true edge if a guide board is fastened to the saw table, as shown above. The saw table can be tilted or level, depending on the width of the board being jointed.

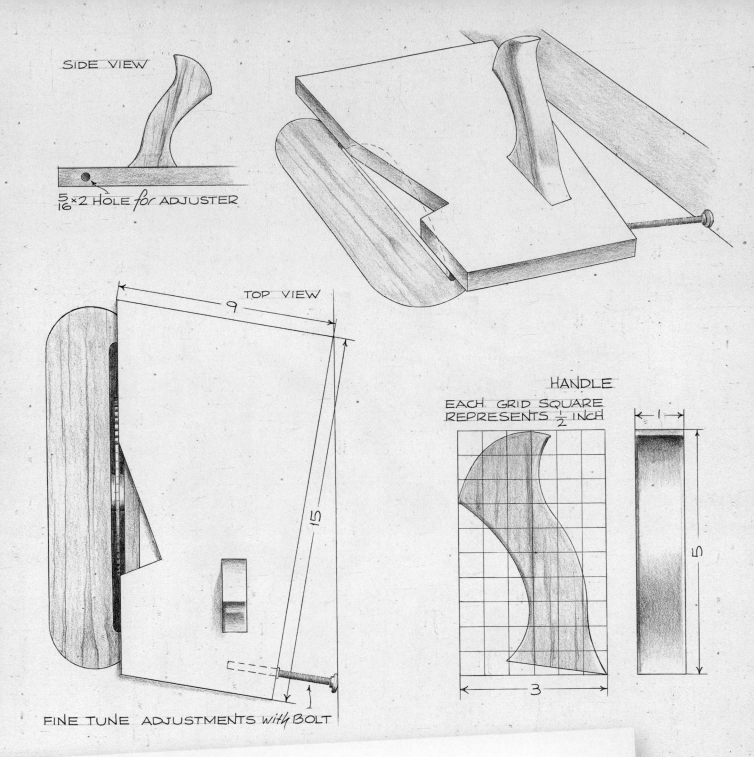

SIDE VIEW

$\frac{5}{16}$ × 2 HOLE *for* ADJUSTER

TOP VIEW

9

15

FINE TUNE ADJUSTMENTS *with* BOLT

HANDLE

EACH GRID SQUARE REPRESENTS $\frac{1}{2}$ INCH

3

1

5

parts list

NO.	COMPONENT	MATERIAL	THICKNESS X WIDTH X LENGTH	
			INCHES	**MILLIMETERS**
1	base plate	melamine	$^3/_4$ × 9 × 15	19 × 229 × 381
1	handle blank	hardwood	$^3/_4$ × 3 × 5	19 × 76 × 127
2	$^1/_4$-20 T-nuts or threaded inserts			
1	$^1/_4$-20 × 4" carriage bolt			
1	$^1/_4$-20 × 2$^1/_2$" flat head machine screw			
1	toggle clamp			
4	#8 × $^3/_4$" self-tapping screws			

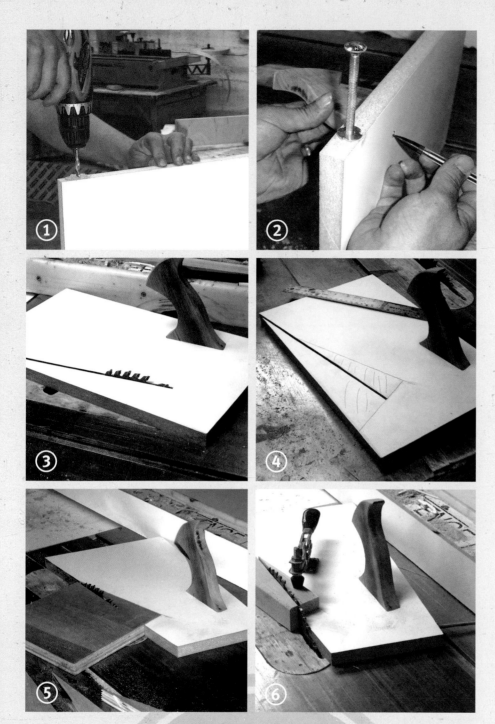

❶ I used a 4" × ¼" bolt for my adjuster. The corresponding threaded insert requires that a $5/16$"-diameter hole be bored about 2" into the edge of the base plate.

❷ Cut the handle using a band saw. To correctly align it on the surface of the base plate, trace its position on the topside of the template, remove the handle and drill a hole approximately in the center of the outline. Reposition the handle and mark the location of the hole on the bottom side of the handle and install the T-nut. If you prefer, a pair of screws would perform equally well, but I liked the security of a beefy bolt holding the handle firmly in place. The T-nut will need to be counter-bored into the bottom of the handle using a spade or Forstner bit.

❸ To layout the bird's mouth, make a cut on the base plate using the table saw blade. The resulting kerf indicates the location of the left-hand side of the wedge.

❹ I used a ruler and a True Angle gauge to locate the right-hand side of the wedge and completed the layout by drawing a line perpendicular to the line on the right-hand side of the wedge. Use a jigsaw or band saw to make the bird's mouth cutout. I made the jig large in order to accommodate different sizes of workpieces.

❺ To set up the jig for the size you need, place the jig on the saw (don't insert the blank just yet) and measure from the blade to the inside edge of the bird's mouth. Set the table saw fence, then use the bolt to fine tune the fixture. When cutting wedges, use your left hand to hold the workpiece steady—use just enough force to advance the workpiece at the same speed as the jig. Flip the blank over after each cut to maximize the yield of wedges from the blank.

❻ The setup is the same when you're cutting tapers—use a ruler and position the jig at the correct distance from the blade. During the cut, your workpiece will remain on the outside (left side) of the blade and the offcut will nestle into the bird's mouth. I recommend using a toggle clamp to secure the offcut. This will support the entire workpiece as you make the cut. Be sure to go completely past the saw blade.

safety tip

The best way to operate this jig is to push it, in one smooth motion, all the way clear of the blade. This will provide the cleanest cuts and most efficient workflow, but it will sever the rear portion of the jig during the first pass over the blade. Should this result in a bird's mouth which is too small for future projects, I recommend simply cutting another one farther into the blank—hence the large 15" × 9" base plate that I use.

BEVELED EDGES ON SQUARE STOCK

I usually bevel the edges of square stock by chucking a 45° bit into a router. The router can then be hand held or installed into a router table. The technique presented in this chapter uses a jointer to achieve the same results.

The basic concept involves a guide block made from a 2×4. The guide block has a V-shaped channel milled into its surface and the workpiece is moved through the channel where it passes over the rotating cutterhead of the jointer. You can adjust the size of the bevel by raising or lowering the infeed table of the jointer.

You can use this technique on almost any stock that has a square corner.

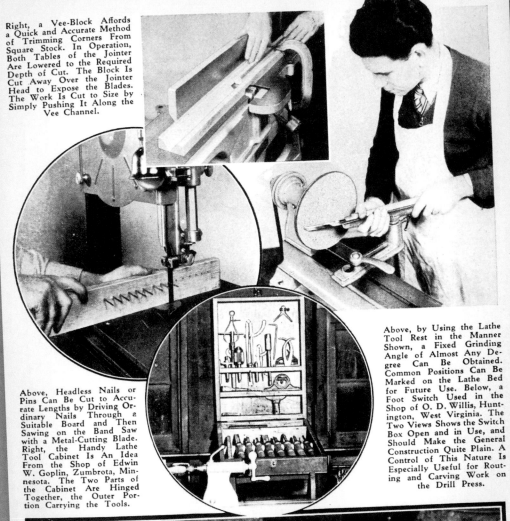

SHOP SUGGESTIONS

Right, a Vee-Block Affords a Quick and Accurate Method of Trimming Corners From Square Stock. In Operation, Both Tables of the Jointer Are Lowered to the Required Depth of Cut. The Block Is Cut Away Over the Jointer Head to Expose the Blades. The Work Is Cut to Size by Simply Pushing It Along the Vee Channel.

Above, Headless Nails or Pins Can Be Cut to Accurate Lengths by Driving Ordinary Nails Through a Suitable Board and Then Sawing on the Band Saw with a Metal-Cutting Blade. Right, the Handy Lathe Tool Cabinet Is An Idea From the Shop of Edwin W. Goplin, Zumbrota, Minnesota. The Two Parts of the Cabinet Are Hinged Together, the Outer Portion Carrying the Tools.

Above, by Using the Lathe Tool Rest in the Manner Shown, a Fixed Grinding Angle of Almost Any Degree Can Be Obtained. Common Positions Can Be Marked on the Lathe Bed for Future Use. Below, a Foot Switch Used in the Shop of O. D. Willis, Huntington, West Virginia. The Two Views Shows the Switch Box Open and in Use, and Should Make the General Construction Quite Plain. A Control of This Nature Is Especially Useful for Routing and Carving Work on the Drill Press.

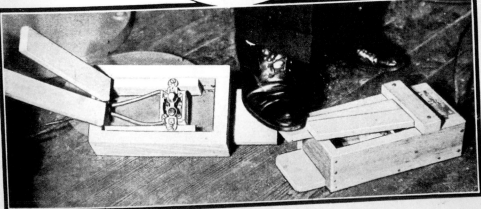

parts list

NO.	COMPONENT	MATERIAL	THICKNESS X WIDTH X LENGTH	
			INCHES	MILLIMETERS
1	V-block	2×4	$1^1/_2 \times 3^1/_2 \times 48$	$38 \times 89 \times 1219$

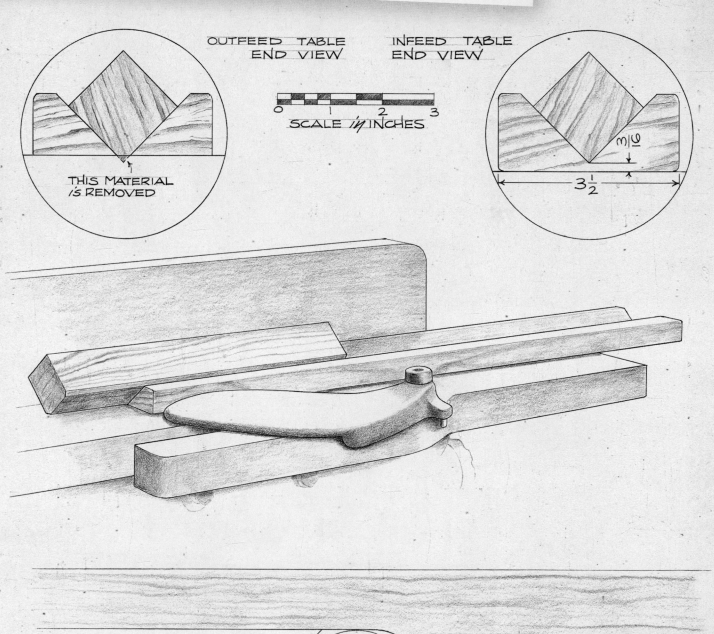

OUTFEED TABLE
END VIEW

INFEED TABLE
END VIEW

THIS MATERIAL
is REMOVED

SCALE in INCHES

0   1   2   3

$3\frac{1}{2}$

$\frac{5}{8}$

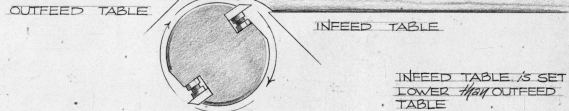

OUTFEED TABLE

INFEED TABLE

INFEED TABLE is SET
LOWER than OUTFEED
TABLE

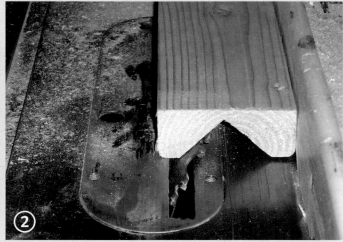

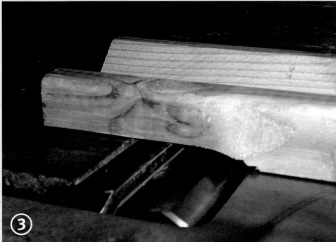

❶ I used a 48″ long 2×4 for the body of the fixture. You may need to flatten the bottom of the 2×4 on the jointer bed if it isn't already flat.

❷ Use a table saw with the blade angled to 45° to cut the V-shaped channel in two passes. The slot should go quite deep into the 2×4—leave about $^3/_{16}$″ untouched on the bottom side.

❸ The original design in the Deltagram required both jointer beds to be lowered equally so that the cutter could be exposed above their surfaces. My jointer only adjusts on the infeed side, so I figured out a way to make the fixture work anyway. My method requires you to carve out the bottom side of the 2×4 for the first four or five inches of its length. You do this by setting the jointer to a depth of $^1/_8$″ and feeding the 2×4 in for those few inches, and then setting the infeed table progressively lower (about $^1/_{16}$″ per pass) until the blade cuts through the bottom into the V-shaped slot. You'll know you're in the ballpark when you see the jointer blade break through into the bottom of the channel.

❹ You can then clamp the fixture to the jointer bed and run a test piece. If you'd like a bigger or smaller cut, just raise or lower the infeed bed accordingly. I have found that this method produces clean, uniform bevels with no taper or snipe at either end. I also recommend this method because it is faster than having to adjust both halves of your jointer table.

❺ This fixture is useful for pieces of various shapes and sizes. In this case, I'm cutting a bevel on the corner of a maple cutting board.

EDGE-SANDING CIRCULAR WORK
ON THE BELT SANDER

I take pride in my ability to cut freehand shapes with the jigsaw, but even with a sharp blade and careful handling of the saw, I usually need to do a little bit of sanding to smooth out the rough spots. This jig is great for truing up circles that you've cut with a band saw or jigsaw, and it works on circles up to 48" in diameter.

The original concept from the 1936 Deltagram offered a neat method of adjustment: it featured a row of holes so that you could place a small pin where you needed it in order to accommodate circles of varying radii. The entire jig could then be moved up or down to fine-tune the settings as needed. While this appears to be perfectly functional, I wanted to see if I could come up with a simpler approach. I ended up cutting a parallel set of saw-kerfs into the lower half of the jig, and mounting a pair of bolts in the upper half. The bolts slide up and down in the kerfs and can be quickly loosened or tightened to achieve the proper height. Instead of using a peg and a series of holes to mount the workpiece, the workpiece simply threads onto an 1¼" screw which I ran through the back side of the upper portion of the jig. It can be moved to any spot you need, with no limit to its adjustability.

My stationary belt sander has four holes tapped into the back side, and I took advantage of them as a place to anchor the jig. In fact, if it hadn't had these holes already, I probably would've taken the time to drill and tap them myself.

Screw-on GRINDING WHEEL ARBOR

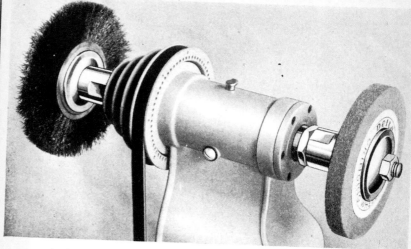

Useful for a Wide Variety of Lathe Operations

No. 144 Right Hand Thread

No. 145 Left Hand Thread

OWNERS of 11-in. Delta lathes will appreciate these new screw-on grinding wheel arbors. They turn on like a faceplate, there's not the slightest chance for anything to come loose in the middle of the job. Both right and left-hand threads are available, the left hand thread fitting the outer end of the lathe spindle. While they are called "grinding wheel arbors," these units can be used for dozens of jobs around the shop. The spindle is ½ in. diameter and will take any wheel, scratch brush, or other tool with ½ in. hole. These arbors are also useful for holding any style of wood chuck, since the standard thread of the spindle can be readily tapped into the back of the chuck.

PRICE EACH

Edge Sanding Circular Work on Belt Sander

PIVOT sanding of circular work on the belt sander can be done with the use of the simple jig shown in the drawing. This consists of a piece of ¾ in. stock measuring about 8 by 12-in. Holes are drilled at 1 in. intervals along the center of the board. The board has two holes in the under edge, into which are tapped two bolts. Corresponding holes, but a close slide fit, are drilled in the edge of the sander fence.

In use, an approximate pivot pin location is selected and the pivot pin (a ¼ in. dowel) is inserted in the hole. The work is fitted to the pin, then the adjusting nuts are turned so that the work comes in contact with the belt. A flat spot is then cut in the work to the right diameter, after which the work is slowly rotated to bring the whole edge to a perfectly circular shape.

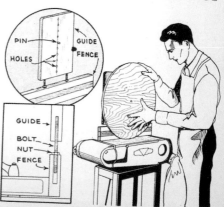

parts list

NO.	COMPONENT	MATERIAL	THICKNESS X WIDTH X LENGTH	
			INCHES	MILLIMETERS
1	lower part	plywood	3/4 × 8 × 18	19 × 203 × 457
1	upper part	plywood	3/4 × 8 × 18	19 × 203 × 457
2	cabinet door pulls with No.8-32 × 1 1/2" machine screws			
4	1/4-20 × 1 1/4" hex-head bolts			

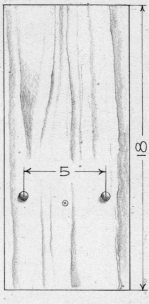

UPPER HALF

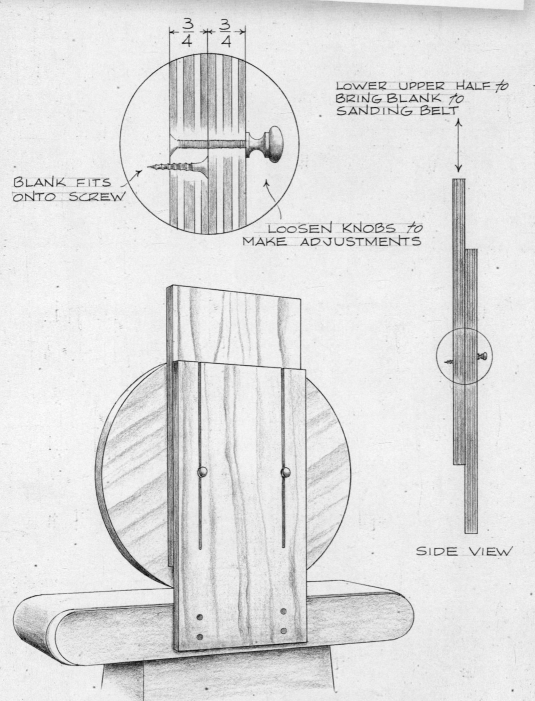

BLANK FITS
ONTO SCREW

LOWER UPPER HALF to
BRING BLANK to
SANDING BELT

LOOSEN KNOBS to
MAKE ADJUSTMENTS

SIDE VIEW

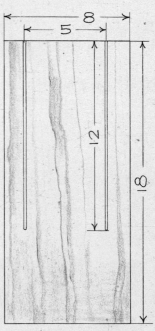

LOWER HALF

❶ Using the table saw, cut two parallel kerfs about 5" apart in the lower part. Saw blades vary in width, so make sure the kerfs will accommodate an $1/8$" bolt. If necessary, move the fence just a bit to cut the kerfs wider.

❷ In the side of your jointer, drill holes and tap them for $1/4$"- 20 bolts.

❸ Measure the locations of the holes and mark them onto the plywood. Once the holes are pre-drilled it is a snap to fasten the lower portion of the jig to the sander.

❹ The upper part of the jig is fastened to the lower portion with a pair of bolts. The holes for these bolts are centered on the saw-kerfs. The holes are countersunk so the bolts' heads are recessed below the surface of the plywood.

❺ Install the pivot screw before the two halves of the jig are assembled.

❻ The knobs on the back side of the jig make adjustments quick and easy.

❼ To use the jig, drill a small hole in back side of the disc. If you've cut the disc using a band saw, the hole will already be there. Fit the disc on the screw, loosen the knobs and lower the upper section of the jig so the disc contacts the sanding belt. Hold the disc firmly and rotate it, sanding the edge. This jig will accommodate discs from 2" to 48" in diameter. For larger discs, locate the pivot screw hinge in the upper part.

The Deltagram

MARCH
1934

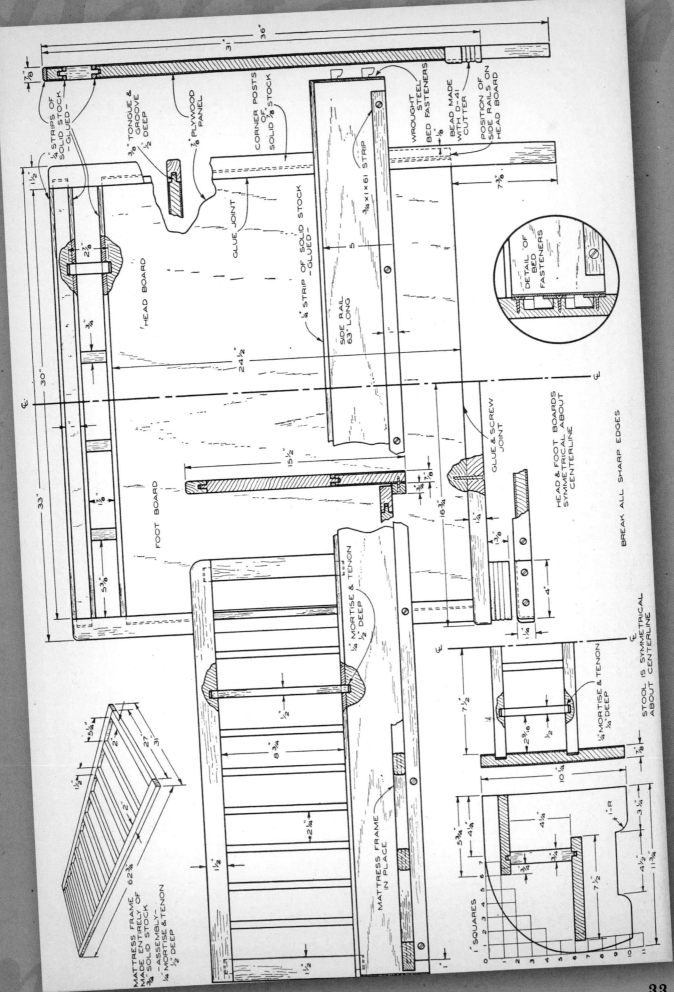

PERFECT CIRCLES ON THE BAND SAW

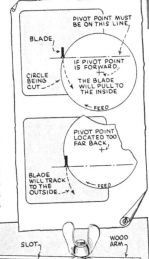

Most woodworkers have a favorite way of laying out and cutting circles. Up until now, however, I had never considered using the band saw for this common workshop task.

The most important thing to realize when building and using this jig is that the position of the pivot point is critical. The pivot point must be set perpendicular to the blade, in such a way that it is even with the front edge of the teeth of the blade. If the pivot point is ahead of or behind the front edge of the teeth, the blade will not track evenly, and you'll end up with a distorted cut through your workpiece. Fortunately, the modifications I have made to the original design make adjustments very easy, so after a few minutes of experimentation, you'll be able to calibrate the jig exactly.

PERFECT CIRCLES
on the Band Saw

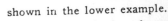

ALL circle-cutting jigs for the band saw or scroll saw feature a pivot point around which the work revolves as it is advanced to the blade. A feature which most craftsmen fail to realize is the importance of the pivot point position in relation to the blade. In order to get perfect circles, this pivot point must be at an exact right angle with the blade, and on a line with the cutting edge or teeth. What happens when this basic rule is not followed is shown in an exaggerated form in the diagram. You will notice that a forward pivot point will cause the blade to track to the inside of the circle being cut, while a pivot point behind the cutting edge of the blade will result in tracking to the outside. A 1/16-in. variation is enough to cause the blade to track, especially if the deviation is back of the blade, as

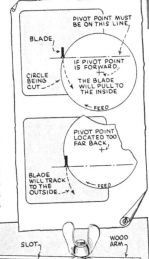

shown in the lower example.

Bearing the basic rule well in mind, you can fashion any number of jigs to more or less conveniently carry the pivot point. Naturally enough, this point should be adjustable so that a wide variety of circle sizes can be cut. A typical jig is shown in the top photo and in the drawing. In this case, the right-hand guide pin is removed, and a longer guide pin of suitable keyway stock substituted. Most band saws have standard 1/2-in. square guides, making the substitution of 1/2-in. keyway stock as perfect as the original set-up. The new guide carries two short studs and one wing nut, as shown, and this portion of the circle-cutting jig can become a permanent part of the band saw. The rest of the jig is simply a hardwood or metal arm which is slotted to take the pivot point. This, the pivot point, can be readily made by cutting off the head of an ordinary bolt and

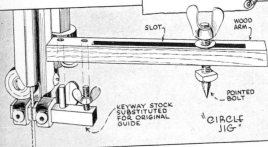

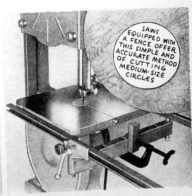

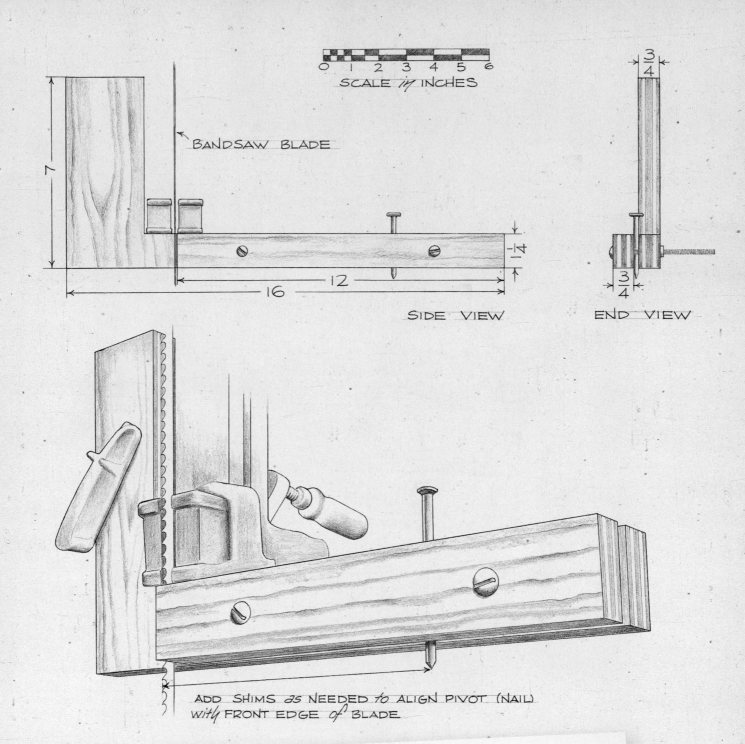

BANDSAW BLADE

SCALE in INCHES

SIDE VIEW

END VIEW

ADD SHIMS as NEEDED to ALIGN PIVOT (NAIL) with FRONT EDGE of BLADE

parts list

NO.	COMPONENT	MATERIAL	THICKNESS X WIDTH X LENGTH	
			INCHES	MILLIMETERS
1	blank for L-brace	plywood	$3/4 \times 7 \times 16$	$19 \times 178 \times 406$
1	front plate	plywood	$3/4 \times 1 1/4 \times 12$	$19 \times 32 \times 305$
2	$1/4$-20 × 3" hex head bolts			
2	$1/4$-20 × 3" hex nuts			
1	nail			
	shims as required			

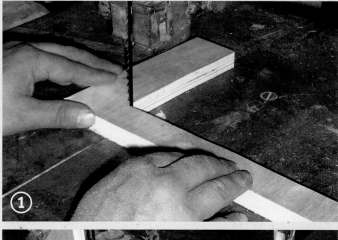

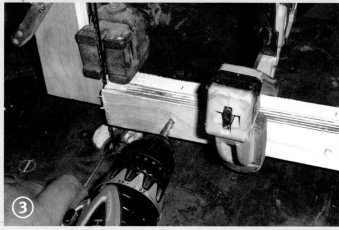

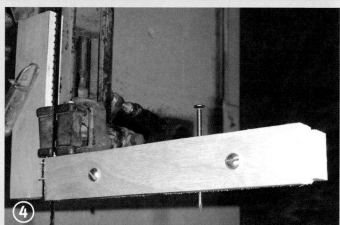

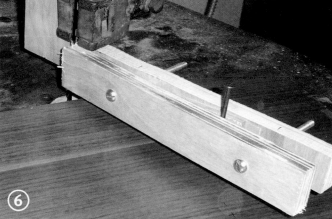

❶ The original design called for an arm that mounted in place of one band saw guide. This didn't work on my band saw, so here's an alternative method. You can decide for yourself exactly how you'd like to mount the jig to your saw, but the principle is the same, regardless. Cut out an L-shaped brace that can be securely clamped to the band saw.

❷ Clamp the front plate on the front of the L-brace.

❸ The front plate is fastened to the brace by a pair of bolts spaced about 7" apart.

❹ A nail squeezed between the front plate and the brace serves as the pivot point for the workpiece.

❺ You may need to shim the nail forward or backward to align it with the front edge of the band saw blade.

❻ To mark the center of the circle on the workpiece, start by making a mark at the center of the workpiece. Then, move 90° to another side, measure the length of the radius from this edge and make another mark. Where these two marks cross is the center of the circle. Place the workpiece so the side you measured the radius from is against the saw blade. Move the workpiece so you can lower the jig with the nail on the center mark. Push the jig down so the nail holds the workpiece, then tighten the jig in place and cut the circle.

SANDING PERFECT POINTS ON DOWELS

7

DOWEL stock can be pointed to any angle by the use of a simple jig block. The block has a hole drilled through it, the hole being a sliding fit for the dowel stock. It is clamped to the sander table at the proper angle. The work is fed to the disk and then rotated.

THIS cabinet for shaper knives keeps all of the various cutters in a convenient location, yet it does not interfere in any way with the operation of the machine. The unit is readily made from plywood and ¾ in. stock to fit the shaper stand.

Idea by Harry Pennington, Jr.
San Antonio, Texas

I've tried to turn points on the ends of dowels by holding them freehand against a moving sander but the results have always been a bit sloppy because I could never manage to hold the dowel firmly and rotate it evenly. This simple fixture provides a stable guide block that can be clamped to a nonmoving part of the sander. It prevents the dowel from jumping around and it allows you to hold the dowel with both hands so that you can control the amount of material being removed.

This fixture can be used on a disc sander or a belt sander if you have a vertical surface on which to support the guide block. Chapter five shows a way to attach a vertical support.

This jig also provides a novel way of sharpening pencils.

parts list

NO.	COMPONENT	MATERIAL	THICKNESS X WIDTH X LENGTH	
			INCHES	MILLIMETERS
1	guide block	2×2	$1^1/_2 \times 1^1/_2 \times 6$	32 × 32 × 152

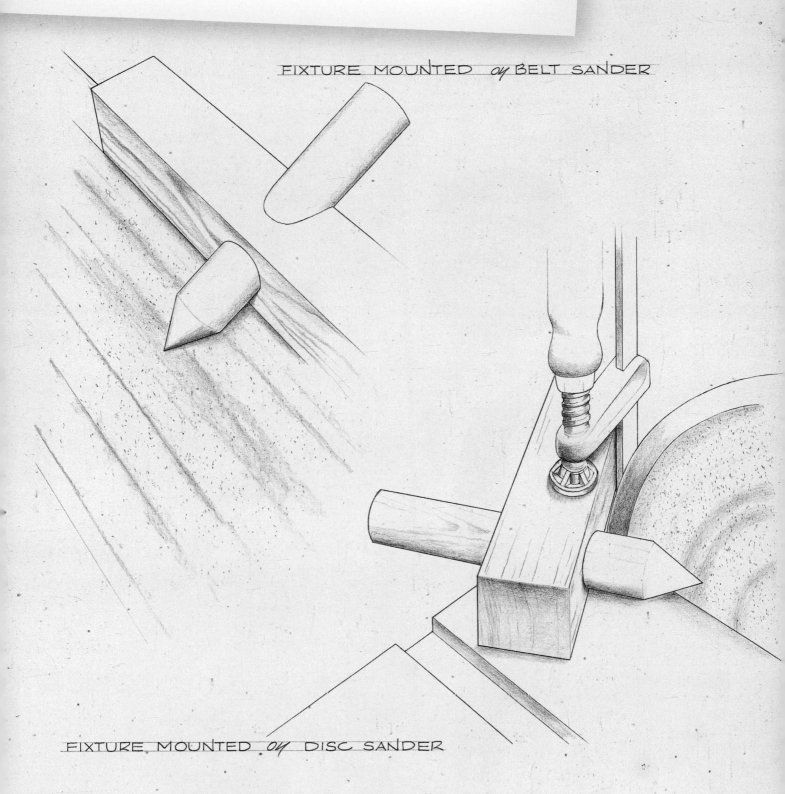

FIXTURE MOUNTED *on* BELT SANDER

FIXTURE MOUNTED *on* DISC SANDER

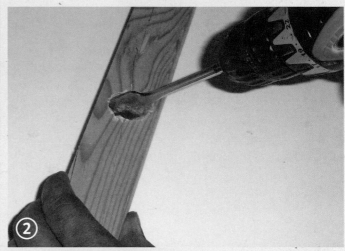

❶ This jig is a guide block with a hole drilled through it. Drill the hole perpendicular to the surface of the guide block. For large diameter holes, I recommend a Forstner or spade bit. An ideal fit will allow the dowel to turn easily but without excess vibration.

❷ If you're making the belt sander version, drill the hole at an angle—the exact angle will depend on the diameter of the dowel and the angle of the point. I suggest trying a couple of different angles to get your desired result.

❸ For the disc-sander, version clamp the guide block directly to the sanding table. If your disc rotates counter clockwise, make sure you mount the block on the left side of the disc so that the sanding motion is down towards the table. If the disc rotates clockwise, clamp the block on the right side of the disc.

❹ For the belt sander version, screw the guide block to a vertical support.

8

SHOP-MADE POCKET HOLE JIG

P ocket holes are getting more and more popular these days, with good reason—they're one of the fastest and easiest ways to securely assemble all sorts of wooden components. I use them on the furniture and cabinets that I build for my clients and also as an integral part of many of my shop-made accessories that help me get my work done.

The original Deltagram suggests holding the workpiece firmly with your hand, but I found that I needed to use a clamp to keep it really secure.

Fastening TABLE TOPS

THE conventional method of fastening table tops by using screws inserted in pocket holes is favored by many craftsmen. The reason is obvious—no extra parts are needed. Pocket holes are easily drilled by using a heavy block of wood with one side bevel ripped at a 15 to 20-degree angle. The work is held against this by hand, as shown in the photo, the guide block setting the required angle and preventing the bit from leading off. In making the original set-up, the location of the guide block is determined by inspection, and should be placed so that the drill centerline intersects center of underedge of work, as shown in photo inset.

The square block method of fastening, Fig. 2, is inexpensive and requires no additional work. Small metal angles, Fig. 3, are practical. The set-down of ⅜ inch applies to solid wood tops; the angle can be butted solid on plywood tops. Wood buttons, Fig. 4, are easily made by rabbeting the end of a ¾ inch thick board to form a 5/16 inch tongue, after which the board is ripped and cross cut to form a number of buttons. Wood buttons for corners should be mitered to allow fastening close to the leg. Standard table top fasteners of 15 gage metal are excellent, Fig. 6. A slight clearance should be allowed at the points shown in Fig. 7—at the top to insure solid fitting; in the groove to permit shrinkage. Similar treatment applies to wood buttons. Allowance for shrinkage in Fig. 3 method is provided by the set-down of the angle. Shrinkage allowance for pocket holes and square block methods is made by drilling screw shank holes slightly oversize.

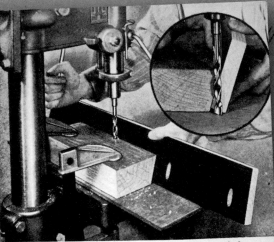

• Pocket holes are easily drilled by using a beveled guide fence. Work should be held firmly to prevent slight kick to left caused by rotation of drill.

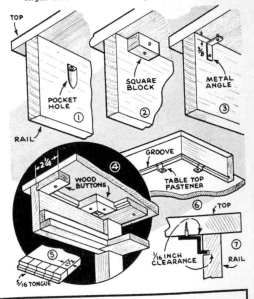

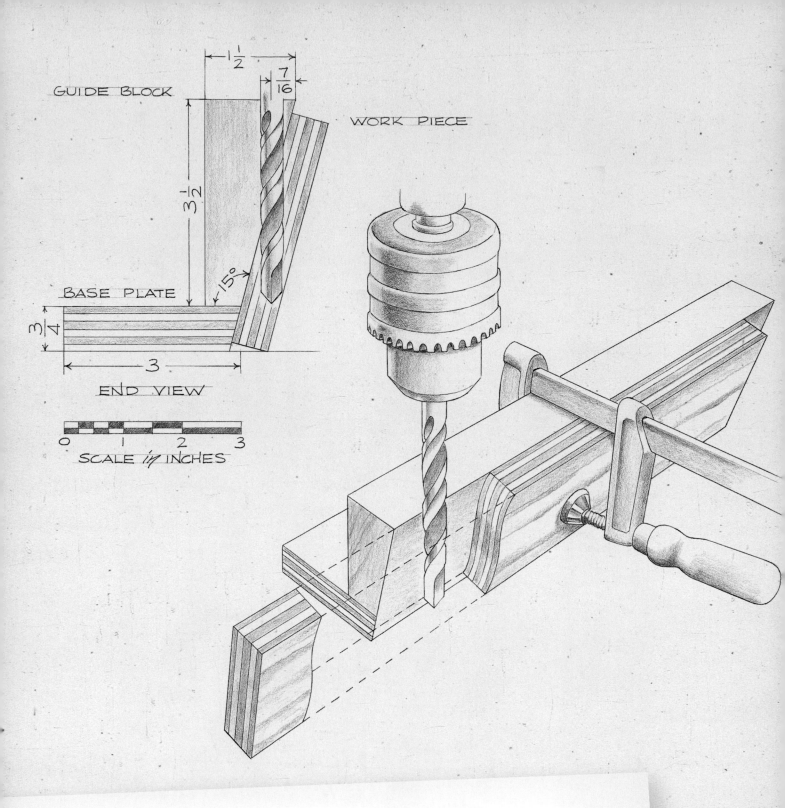

GUIDE BLOCK

$1\frac{1}{2}$

$\frac{7}{16}$

WORK PIECE

$3\frac{1}{2}$

BASE PLATE

$\frac{3}{4}$

15°

3

END VIEW

0   1   2   3

SCALE in INCHES

parts list

		THICKNESS X WIDTH X LENGTH	
NO. COMPONENT	MATERIAL	INCHES	MILLIMETERS
1 guide block	2×4	$1\frac{1}{2} \times 3\frac{1}{2} \times 12$	38 × 89 × 305
1 base plate	plywood	$\frac{3}{4} \times 3 \times 12$	19 × 76 × 305

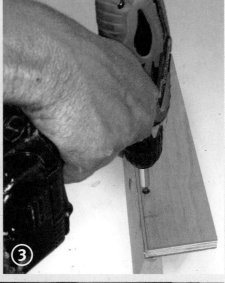

❶ This jig has a guide block with its front face ripped to 15 to 20°. (The commercially made jig that I own is set up for a 15° angle.)

❷ Rip the front edge of the cleat at a 15° angle so it lines up flush with the guide block.

❸ Use glue and screws to secure the guide block to the cleat.

❹ The center of the $7/16$" drill bit should be in $7/16$" from the front of the guide block. Clamp the cleat to the drill press table. Adjust the stops on the drill press so the bit bottoms out $3/4$" above the surface of the drill press table.

❺ With the jig in place, clamp the workpiece to the front of the guide block and drill the first pocket hole. Once the first hole is cut, move the workpiece as necessary to cut a row of pocket holes. I have found this jig works as well as the commercial jig I use on a daily basis. The only difference is that this jig does not cut a pilot hole for the screw. This can be remedied by using a stepped drill bit.

❻ The pocket holes align nicely and are free of tear-out.

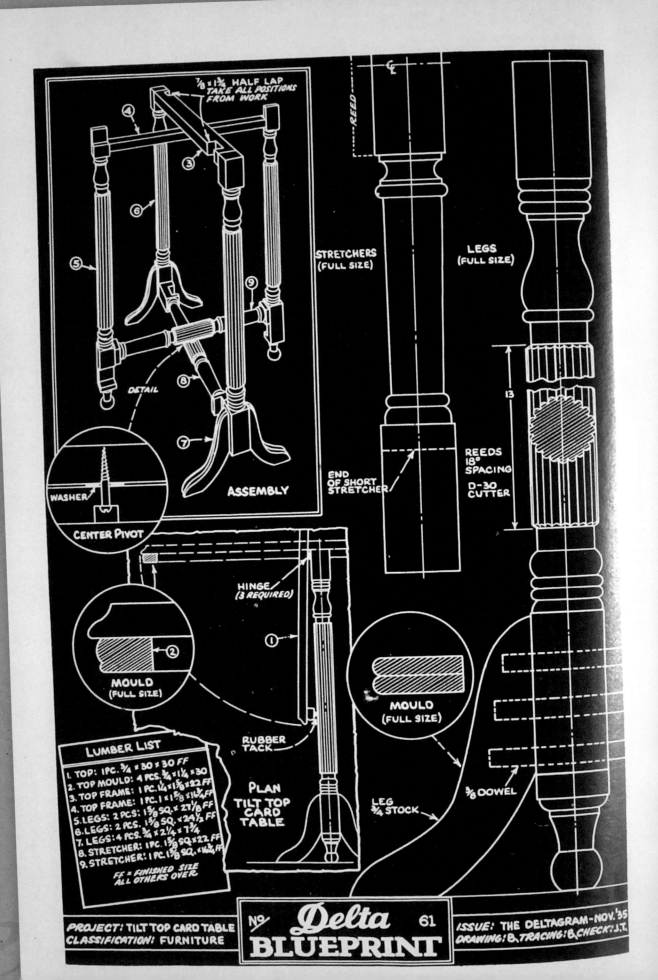

7/8 x 1 3/4 HALF LAP
TAKE ALL POSITIONS
FROM WORK

REED

STRETCHERS
(FULL SIZE)

LEGS
(FULL SIZE)

13

REEDS
18° SPACING
D-30 CUTTER

END OF SHORT STRETCHER

DETAIL

WASHER

CENTER PIVOT

ASSEMBLY

HINGE
(3 REQUIRED)

MOULD
(FULL SIZE)

MOULD
(FULL SIZE)

LEG 3/4 STOCK

3/8 DOWEL

RUBBER TACK

PLAN
TILT TOP
CARD
TABLE

LUMBER LIST

1. TOP: 1 PC. 3/4 x 30 x 30 FF
2. TOP MOULD: 4 PCS. 3/4 x 1 1/4 x 30
3. TOP FRAME: 1 PC. 1/4 x 1 5/8 x 22 FF
4. TOP FRAME: 1 PC. 1 x 1 5/8 x 16 3/4 FF
5. LEGS: 2 PCS. 1 5/8 SQ. x 27 7/8 FF
6. LEGS: 2 PCS. 1 5/8 SQ. x 24 1/2 FF
7. LEGS: 4 PCS. 3/4 x 2 1/4 x 7 3/4
8. STRETCHER: 1 PC. 1 5/8 SQ x 22 FF
9. STRETCHER: 1 PC. 1 5/8 SQ. x 14 1/2 FF

FF = FINISHED SIZE
ALL OTHERS OVER

PROJECT: TILT TOP CARD TABLE
CLASSIFICATION: FURNITURE

No. 61 *Delta* BLUEPRINT

ISSUE: THE DELTAGRAM—NOV. '35
DRAWING: B. TRACING: B. CHECK: J.T.

46

TILT TOP CARD TABLE

WHILE offering little difficulties in the way of construction, this table presents a very smart appearance when properly made and finished. Start by making the six turnings required. These arc shown full-size on the original blueprint, or you can scale the small drawing on the opposite page and multiply by 2.5 to arrive at the proper dimensions. The reeding on the legs and stretchers is easily run in on the drill press, using D-30 or D-31 shaper cutter in connection with a simple jig to hold the work level, as shown in the lower photo. The work should first be marked on the lathe, using the dividing head, so that accurate spacing will be assured.

Make the band sawed legs next, and then set up the various pieces in a temporary assembly. Care in measuring is required at this point, and the various interlocking half-lap joints should not be cut until an actual set-up determines their position.

The top is made from select ¾-in. plywood, with an outside rail bringing up the total edge thickness to 1½ in. The rail pieces are neatly mitered at the corners, this operation being done after the stock is moulded to shape. Fastening is by means of glue and screws into the top proper. An inlay banding on the top surface adds considerably to its appearance. If the table is being constructed for a paint or lacquer finish, the top surface offers unlimited possibilities for decoration. In any case, a rich top surface is essential since this type of table does double duty as both table and screen, both roles focusing attention on the top.

The final assembly of top to frame is by means of three hinges spaced equally across the center of the top, as shown in the detail. Check the position of the underside of the rail against the legs when the table is folded, and insert a rubber tack in the rail at the two contact points as a check against marring. Lighter plywood can be used for the top providing a heavy edge moulding and stiffening cross members are used in making a suitable framework.

This Tilt Top Table Does Double Duty as Card Table and Screen, as Shown in the Upper Photos. Photo Directly Above Pictures the Reeding of the Turned Legs on the Drill Press.

9

FAST-ACTION DRILL PRESS TABLE

Once you've used this fixture, you'll probably wonder how you ever worked without it. It provides a high level of precision, adjustability and gives consistent results every time. It is easy to install and remove and is suitable for aligning and securing workpieces of many shapes and sizes.

I recommend making or buying a couple of toggle clamps to hold down workpieces. Angled blocks can be made to correctly position non-square workpieces. The Shop-Made Pocket Hole Jig (chapter eight), works great with this fixture as do sanding drums chucked in the drill press.

Shop IDEAS

Magnet Sets Jointer Knives

JOINTER knives, after being removed from the head for grinding, can be reset quickly and accurately by using a magnet in the manner shown in the photo and drawing. An index mark should be scribed near the end of the magnet, each blade to be set to this mark. Another mark or some fixed clamping arrangement is necessary to place the first mark at the highest point of knife travel. Each knife is placed in its slot and is immediately pulled up to the required level by the magnet, after which the setscrews are tightened. It will be noted that this method of working not only makes mounting convenient, but automatically aligns the blades flush with the rear table.

Brush Eliminates Saw Dust

SAW DUST can be prevented from accumulating on both upper and lower wheels of the band saw by installing a small stiff brush in the position shown. This idea is particularly useful for production work in yellow pine or other resinous wood.

Fast-Action Drill Table

REGULAR users of the wood drill press table will appreciate the merits of this method of mounting. The table can be put on or taken off in a fraction of the time required to set the four standard mounting bolts. The photo shows an under view of the table, while the diagram shows the table in place. The wingnut bolt can be obtained from a small ten-cent clamp, and should be inclined ever so slightly so that it will have a tendency to draw the wood table down. All-metal construction with angle iron can be substituted if desired.

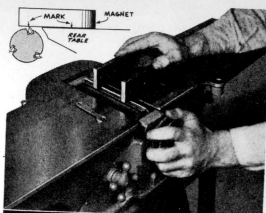

MARK — MAGNET — REAR TABLE

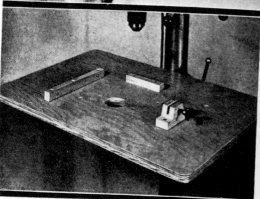

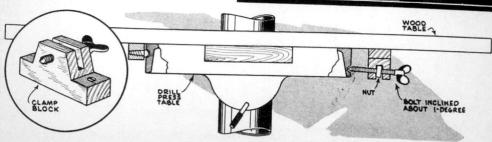

WOOD TABLE

CLAMP BLOCK

DRILL PRESS TABLE

NUT

BOLT INCLINED ABOUT 1-DEGREE

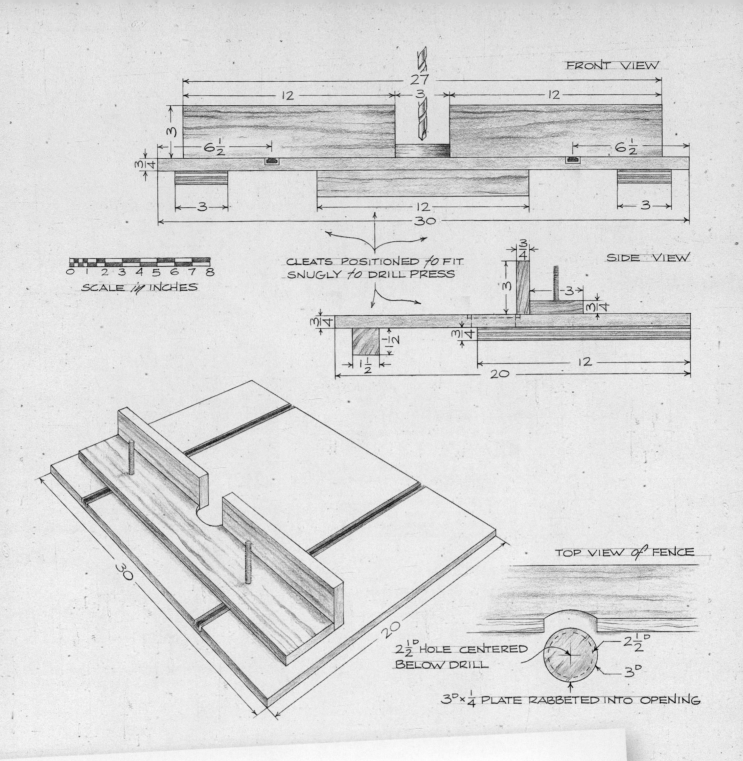

FRONT VIEW

27

12   3   12

3

6½   6½

¾

3   3

12

30

SCALE in INCHES
0 1 2 3 4 5 6 7 8

CLEATS POSITIONED to FIT
SNUGLY to DRILL PRESS

SIDE VIEW

¾

3   3

¾   ¾

3

¾   1½

1½

20   12

TOP VIEW of FENCE

2½ᴰ HOLE CENTERED
BELOW DRILL

2½ᴰ

3ᴰ

3ᴰ × ¼ PLATE RABBETED INTO OPENING

30

20

parts list

NO.	COMPONENT	MATERIAL	THICKNESS X WIDTH X LENGTH	
			INCHES	MILLIMETERS
1	deck	melamine	³/₄ × 20 × 30	19 × 508 × 762
1	fence base	plywood	³/₄ × 3 × 27	19 × 76 × 686
2	front strips for fence	plywood	³/₄ × 3 × 12	19 × 76 × 305
1	aluminum T-track		48 L	1219 L
2	¹/₄-20 × 1¹/₂" T-slot bolts			
2	hold-down clamps			
2	star knobs			

❶ Melamine makes a good base because its bright white surface reflects light and makes everything you're working with stand out as highly visible. The deck will need to be fitted with a device that allows it to be installed and removed quickly and easily and remain precisely aligned during all phases of operation. For my drill press, I installed a series of cleats on the underside of the deck so that it can simply be pressed into place from above. Make the fit snug.

❷ With the deck in position, I marked the spot directly below the chuck.

❸ Centered on this mark, I drilled a $2^{1}/2$"-diameter hole that will allow sanding drums to be recessed below the surface of the deck.

❹ The hole needs to be rabbeted to accept a $^{1}/4$"-thick cover plate. The cover plate will create a flat, even work surface and can be easily replaced if it becomes damaged or worn. It can be bandsawn from scrap $^{1}/4$" plywood.

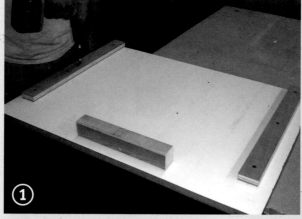

❺ The key to the utility of this fixture is a set of parallel T-tracks which are laid flush with the surface of the deck. The exact placement of the tracks isn't critical—I centered them $6^{1}/2$" from each edge—but they do need to be exactly parallel. The tracks are available from most woodworking specialty stores and catalogs and can accommodate a range of different hold-downs, clamps and accessories.

❻ Center the fence's base on the table and cut a 3"-wide and 1"-deep curved notch in the center of the fence's base. This notch will provide space to position the fence around a sanding drum or Microplane (see Suppliers). Drill $^{5}/16$" holes so the $^{3}/16$" mounting bolts have a bit of wiggle room.

❼ Attach the two face plates to the bottom using countersunk screws.

❽ The assembled fence is attached to the fence base with bolts and knobs. To take things a step further, you can shim the left front strip out by $^{1}/32$" or $^{1}/16$" (use double-sided tape for this). You now have a safe and precise jointer for flattening or thicknessing small stock.

CURVED FORMS
FOR THE STATIONARY BELT SANDER

This tool takes some time to build, so it's probably not worth the effort if you've only got one or two pieces to sand, but it really shines when you need to make a number of identical pieces quickly.

A standard 48" × 6" belt only deflects about 2" to 2½" when the tension is loosened. This may be enough for really shallow curves, but in my experience, you'll probably need to get a larger sanding belt. I found a local shop with 54" belts on hand and a couple of abrasives suppliers were willing to make up custom sizes, so this didn't end up being an obstacle.

FORMS for Belt Sanding

WHILE the belt sander is intended and most extensively used for sanding flat surfaces, it can be used with perfect success for finishing curved work. This is done with the use of forms. In most cases, the operation is practical only in production runs of at least ten pieces in order to justify the cost and time involved in making the required form.

Fig. 1 illustrates a simple job set-up. In this case, the work to be finished has an edge which is a part of a

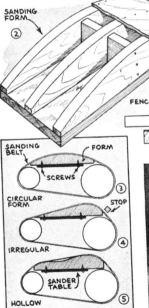

true circle. The form is built to this same circular arc, and is fastened by means of machine screws to the sander table. Since the work is circular, there is no need for any stop device, the track of the sanding belt being to the same curve at any point over the surface of the jig. An irregular form, as shown in Fig. 4, has a different curve at every point. It can be seen, therefore, that a stop block must be used so that the work can be placed against the belt in the proper position. The hollow form, Fig. 5, can be used for concave curves up to about one inch deep. The belt should be run fairly slack so that pressure by the work will cause it to assume the required shape.

Certain types of moulded edges can be worked with the use of forms, a typical example being the rounded corner. The form for this mould is simply a groove down the center of a flat piece of wood, as shown in Fig. 7. The fence is adjusted so that the edge to be worked is directly over the groove, as shown in Fig. 6. Pressing down on the work will force the belt into contact with the form and thus

The use of regular sanding belts over forms and shredded paper without backing adds to the scope of work which can be done on the belt sander.

sand the edge to the required shape. A certain nicety of touch in knowing just when to lift the work must be acquired by experience. Ogee curves and thumb moulds can be worked in the same manner. The regular type of sanding belt can be used, but where the mould assumes a more complex shape, a special lightweight backing must be used to give the belt the required flexibility.

The utmost in flexibility in a sanding belt is obtained by the use of slashed or shredded cloth back belts. This abrasive belting is commonly obtained in a width of 4 inches. It is slashed into narrow ribbons about ⅛-inch wide, the ribbons being held together by means of short sections of uncut belt, as can be seen in Fig. 8. This belt can be used over a form, or, it can be run without backing, as in Fig. 8. When run without backing, it is somewhat simpler to remove the back plate of the sander rather than the sanding table. Where the tilting sanding table is to be used, however, it is necessary to remove the main sanding table. Belts of this kind are ideal for finished castings featuring all-over curved surfaces.

parts list

NO.	COMPONENT	MATERIAL	THICKNESS X WIDTH X LENGTH		COMMENTS
			INCHES	**MILLIMETERS**	
2	form sides	scrap	$^3/_4 \times 5 \times 12$	19 × 127 × 305	Note that the dimensions listed will vary depending on the size of the
1	skin	plywood	$^1/_8 \times 6 \times 24$	3 × 152 × 610	forms you require. You may also need some scrap stock to build up the
1	form bottom	scrap	$^3/_4 \times 6 \times 12$	19 × 152 × 305	bottom of the form so it fits snugly underneath the sanding belt.
5	risers	scrap	$^3/_4 \times 6 \times 12$	19 × 152 × 305	
	custom-size belts				

You can also look for odd-size belts at machinery and woodworking suppliers. I found a 54" belt, which I substituted for the stock 48" belt.

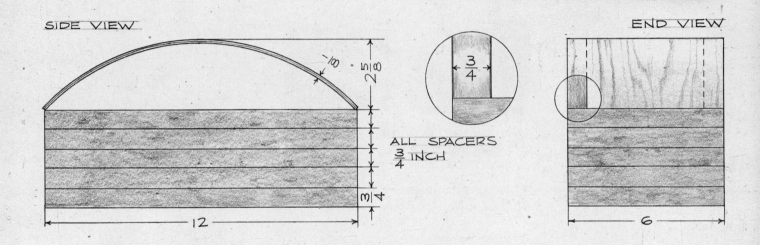

SIDE VIEW

ALL SPACERS $\frac{3}{4}$ INCH

END VIEW

FORM MOUNTED
on BELT SANDER

❶ To make a pattern for the forms, use the finished piece for a pattern and trace onto the form stock.

❷ Subtract $1/8$" from the top side of the pattern to account for the $1/8$" thick plywood skin. Using a compass, trace the top line of the form.

❸ Once you've cut out one form side on the band saw, use this side as a template for the other side.

❹ Attach the bottom plate using glue and nails or countersunk screws.

❺ The skin can be glued and nailed to the top. If you're having trouble getting it to bend easily, you can use thinner layers. I soaked my $1/8$" plywood in water for about 10 minutes before assembly and it was easy to bend.

❻ Build up the bottom side of the form as needed so the belt fits snugly. The total height of this form was $7^1/4$".

❼ The form is slid into the space between the belt and the platen. It does not need to be secured in any way, as the tension on the belt will hold it in place. If the belt doesn't move easily, make the form a little shorter. If it is too loose, make the form a little taller.

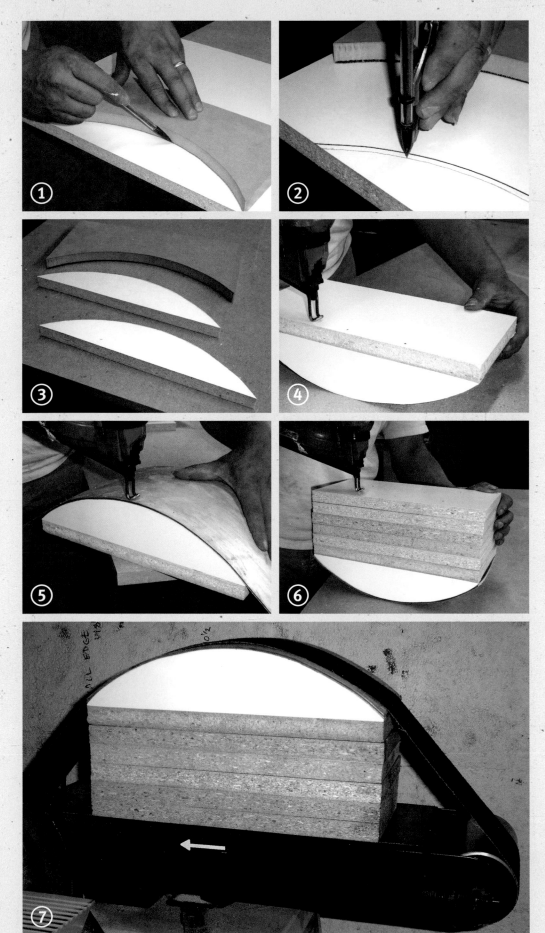

DISK SANDER PIVOTING JIG

11

Even if you've got the skill or tooling to cut out near-perfect circles, you'll usually need to do some sanding to remove blade marks or to smooth irregularities. This jig can be built in under a half an hour and it can handle circles up to a 20" diameter.

The jig consists of a base plate that can be easily affixed to the worktable on your disk sander. A set of cleats on the underside ensures consistent positioning and a clamp holds it securely in place. The base plate is fitted with a sliding strip which holds an indexing pin. The pin fits into a hole on the bottom side of the center of the workpiece and the sliding strip can be adjusted to fit the radius you need. I use a spring clamp to lock down the sliding strip.

Using PIVOT JIG on Disk Sander

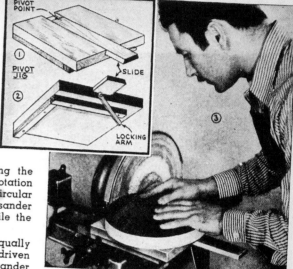

CIRCULAR work which is to be sanded should always be worked with the use of a pivot jig. Top and bottom views of a simple jig are shown in Figs. 1 and 2. Cleats on the underside provide a positive stop against the front and side of the standard table. The sliding strip can be set at any position, and is locked in place by pushing down on the locking lever, the end of which works like a cam. In use, the work is first band sawed to shape, after which it is mounted on the pivot point. The sliding strip is locked at the required distance from the sanding disk. Pushing the table into the disk sets the cut, and rotation finishes the entire edge to a perfect circular shape. The jig can be clamped to the sander table or simply held with one hand while the other hand rotates the work.

Any other style of pivot jig will work equally well, the simplest set-up being a brad driven into a board which is clamped to the sander table at the required distance from the sanding disk. An overhead pivot point, as shown at the right, can be made from circular saw hold-down parts. This type of jig is fully adjustable and has the advantage of a visible pivot point which can be accurately set in the center of the work.

The sanding of corners is allied to circular work in that the edge being worked is part of a true circle. Most work of this nature can be done freehand, sweeping the corner of the work across the face of the sanding disk two or three times until the desired round is obtained. More accurate results are possible if the pivot jig is used in the manner shown in the drawings at the bottom of the page. In use, the sliding strip is first locked in place at the required distance from the face of the sanding disk. A pencil mark is then drawn on the table of the jig, this mark being the same distance from the pivot point as the pivot point is from the sanding disk, as shown in Fig. 4. The work is placed against a guide fastened to the rear edge of the jig, as shown in Fig. 5, and is brought down on the pivot point in alignment with the pencil mark. Rotating the work rounds the corner, see Fig. 6. Fig. 7 shows how the jig table can be marked

A pivot jig is almost a necessity in sanding circular pieces if accurate work is to be done.

with pencil lines as a guide to placing work of any radius. Lines are drawn on the table at a 45 degree angle. Where these lines touch the edge of the table, other lines are brought down. Set to any mark, the pivot will be equally spaced from mark and disk.

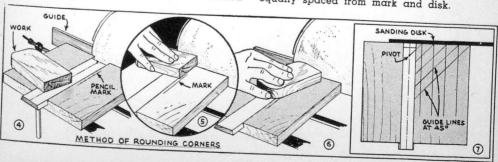

METHOD OF ROUNDING CORNERS

parts list

NO.	COMPONENT	MATERIAL	THICKNESS X WIDTH X LENGTH	
			INCHES	MILLIMETERS
1	base plate	plywood	$^3/_4 \times 12 \times 12$	$19 \times 305 \times 305$
1	sliding strip	hardwood	$^7/_{16} \times 2 \times 12$	$11 \times 51 \times 305$
1	bottom cleat	MDF	$^3/_4 \times 1 \times 12$	$19 \times 25 \times 305$
1	side cleat	MDF	$^3/_4 \times 1^1/_2 \times 12$	$19 \times 38 \times 305$
	rivet or nail for the indexing pin			

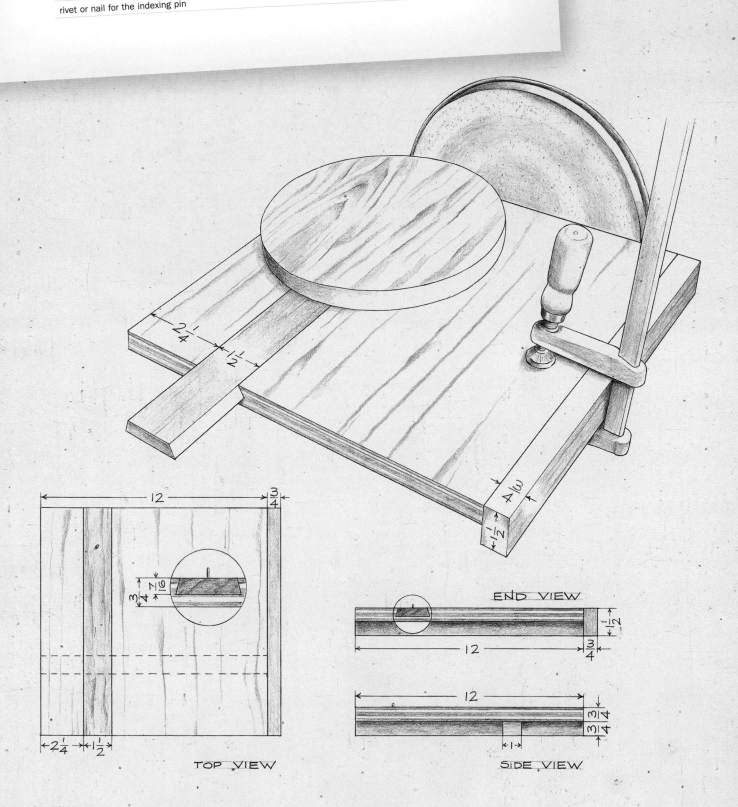

TOP VIEW

END VIEW

SIDE VIEW

❶ The dovetailed groove starts out as a dado cut 1¹/₂" wide and ⁷/₁₆" deep. You can cut this dado with a router table or table saw.

❷ I used a 14° dovetail bit in my router table to cut the sloped sides of the groove.

❸ I suggest cutting the sliding strip slightly wider than necessary so that it can be fit snugly in the groove—it shouldn't be too loose. I used the table saw to rip the strip to width. Each edge has a 14° bevel. The pin is fit into a hole that is drilled about 2" from the end of the strip. For the pin I used a rivet trimmed to length. A brad nail will also work as a pin.

❹ Two cleats hold the base plate in place. One attaches to the bottom of the base plate and the other attaches to its right-hand edge. Remember to locate the table so the sanding action is at the downward rotation of the sanding disc.

❺ To operate the jig, clamp it in place and place the workpiece onto the pin. Push the workpiece toward the sanding disc until it is lightly touching. Use a spring clamp to hold the sliding strip in place.

The Deltagram

A "DELTA-CRAFT" PUBLICATION

USEFUL JIGS FOR THE SHOP

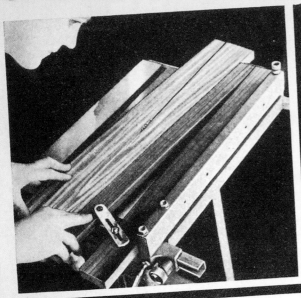

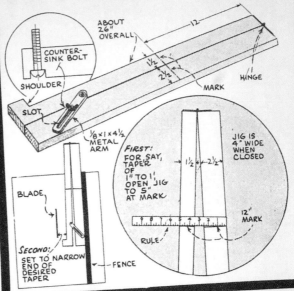

ABOUT 26" OVERALL

COUNTER-SINK BOLT

SHOULDER

SLOT

$1/8 \times 1 \times 4 1/2$ METAL ARM

12

1/2

2 1/2

MARK

HINGE

BLADE

SECOND: SET TO NARROW END OF DESIRED TAPER

FIRST: FOR SAY, TAPER OF 1" TO 1' OPEN JIG TO 5" AT MARK

FENCE

JIG IS 4" WIDE WHEN CLOSED

1 1/2 2 1/2

RULE

12" MARK

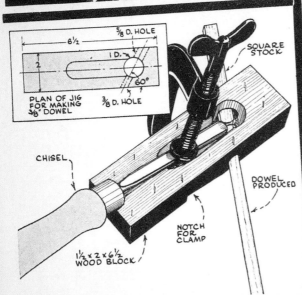

6 1/2

5/8 D. HOLE

2

1 D.

60°

PLAN OF JIG FOR MAKING 3/8" DOWEL

3/8 D. HOLE

SQUARE STOCK

CHISEL

DOWEL PRODUCED

NOTCH FOR CLAMP

$1 1/2 \times 2 \times 6 1/2$ WOOD BLOCK

The top photograph and drawing show a tapering jig idea from the shop of Doctor D. C. Morton, Richmond, Virginia. This is similar to the jig described in The Deltagram for November, 1934, excepting that the hinge is reversed. The jig should be made to some exact width, say, 4 in. In setting, the amount of taper to the foot is measured on the 12 in. line; then, the jig is placed against the fence and the shoulder set to the narrow end of the desired taper. ● A clever dowel jig by Mr. T. Ostbye, Fargo, North Dakota, is shown at the center. The jig can be used on either the lathe or the drill press, and larger or smaller units can be made up to accommodate different sizes. The round hole through which the square stock is inserted should be of an exact diameter equal to the diagonal of the stock used. ● Mr. Harold C. Slone, Flint, Michigan, offers the excellent saw fixture idea shown at the left. The shelf is held by metal brackets, and offers plenty of space for tool accessories, while a cabinet under the shelf provides room for saw blades.

CUTTING LONG MITERS WITH A STRAIGHT BIT
ON THE ROUTER TABLE

This jig provides a neat way of cutting long miters. Because it uses a router bit and not a saw blade, it produces smooth, finished quality edges that require no sanding. It is adjustable to any angle between 0 and 90° and it can be easily installed and removed from your router tabletop. It requires a longer than usual router bit—I used a bit with a 2½" cutting edge. With the deck in the flat position, this jig can also be used as a jointer.

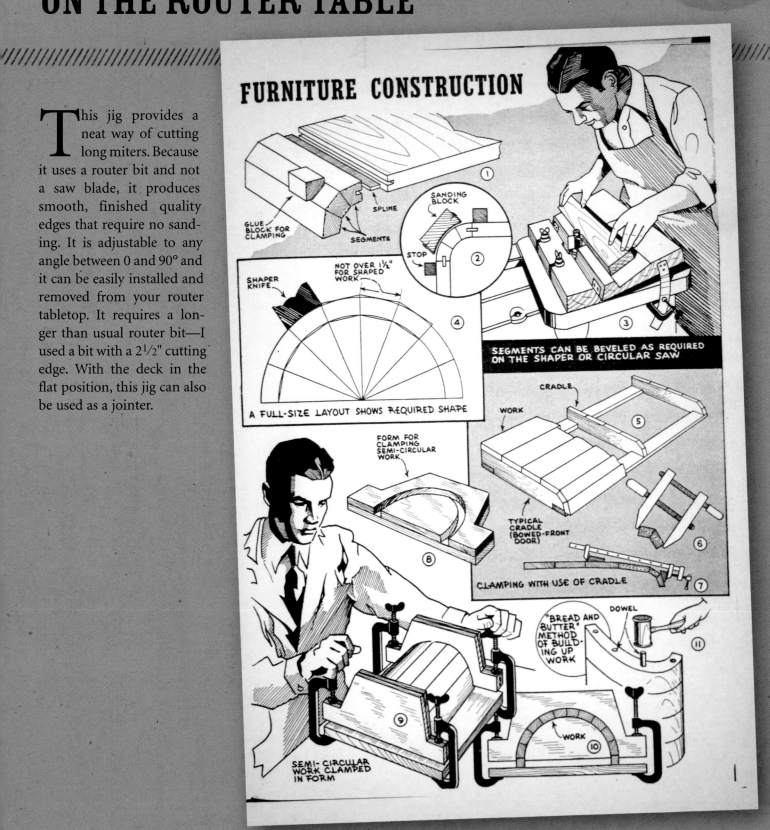

FURNITURE CONSTRUCTION

GLUE BLOCK FOR CLAMPING
SPLINE
SEGMENTS
1

SANDING BLOCK
STOP
2

3

SEGMENTS CAN BE BEVELED AS REQUIRED ON THE SHAPER OR CIRCULAR SAW

SHAPER KNIFE
NOT OVER 1½" FOR SHAPED WORK
4
A FULL-SIZE LAYOUT SHOWS REQUIRED SHAPE

CRADLE
WORK
5
TYPICAL CRADLE (BOWED-FRONT DOOR)
6
CLAMPING WITH USE OF CRADLE
7

FORM FOR CLAMPING SEMI-CIRCULAR WORK
8

"BREAD AND BUTTER" METHOD OF BUILDING UP WORK
DOWEL
11

9

WORK
10

SEMI-CIRCULAR WORK CLAMPED IN FORM

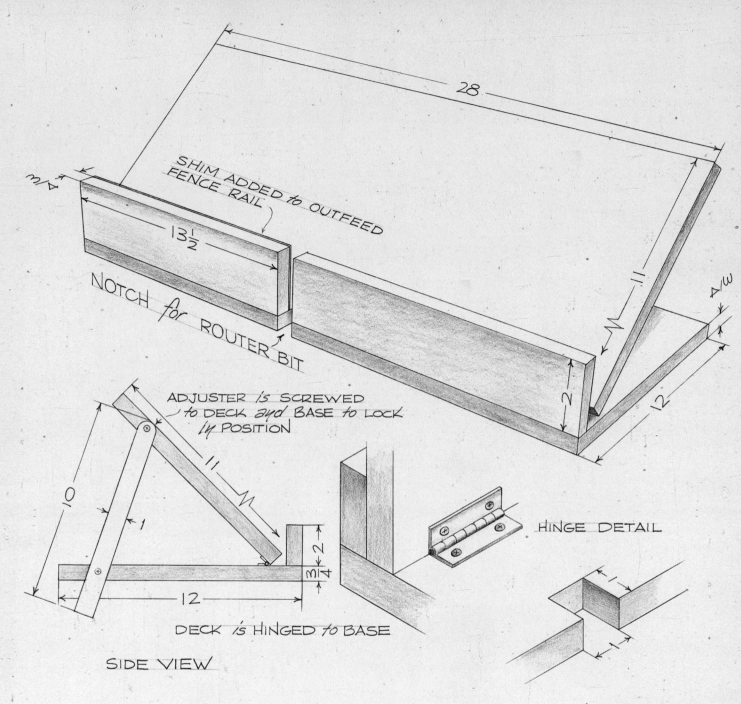

SHIM ADDED to OUTFEED FENCE RAIL

28

3/4

13½

NOTCH for ROUTER BIT

11

2

3/4

12

ADJUSTER is SCREWED to DECK and BASE to LOCK in POSITION

10

1

11

2

3/4

12

DECK is HINGED to BASE

SIDE VIEW

HINGE DETAIL

1

1

NOTCH DETAIL

parts list

NO.	COMPONENT	MATERIAL	THICKNESS X WIDTH X LENGTH	
			INCHES	MILLIMETERS
1	deck	melamine	$3/4 \times 11 \times 28$	$19 \times 279 \times 711$
1	base	particleboard	$3/4 \times 12 \times 28$	$19 \times 305 \times 711$
2	fence rails	MDF	$3/4 \times 2 \times 13^{1}/_{2}$	$19 \times 51 \times 343$
1	adjuster	scrap	$1/4 \times 1 \times 10$	$6 \times 25 \times 254$
2	surface mount butt hinges			

❶ Once the deck and base panels are cut out, cut a 1" × 1" notch in the base with a jigsaw.

❷ The fence rails can be attached at this point—take your time because the rails need to run in a perfectly straight line. I used super glue to hold them in place, then reinforced the joint with countersunk screws inserted from the bottom of the base.

❸ The hinges can be screwed into both the base and the deck. Allow a gap of about $1/2$" between the leading edge of the deck and the fence rails.

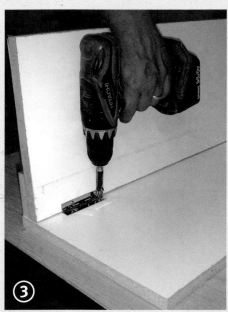

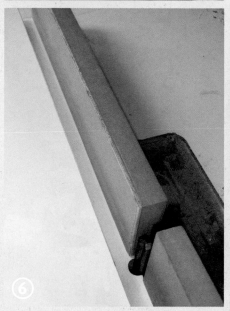

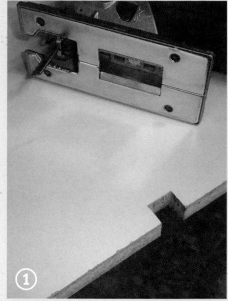

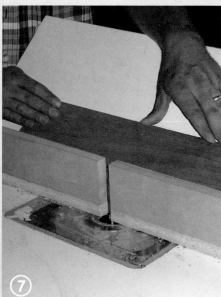

❹ Use a piece of scrap stock screwed into the edges of the deck and the bases as an adjuster. I used an angle finder to set the deck to the desired angle.

❺ Either screw or clamp the base to the table. The router bit should protrude about $1/8$" past the fence rails.

❻ The outfeed fence is shimmed flush to the router bit to ensure the stock will feed properly. I used superglue to tack down the $1/8$"-thick shim.

❼ Looking from the front of the router table, feed the stock left to right. This is a safe and easy operation.

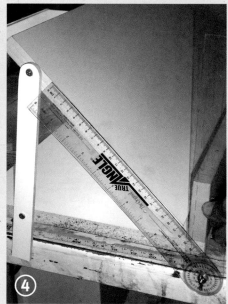

13

SANDING WORKPIECES TO PRECISE WIDTHS
ON THE TABLE SAW

This easy-to-build tool comes in handy in my shop. The concept is both simple and effective—I'm surprised that I had never seen it done before.

Stick-on sanding discs are available in different diameters—I chose to use 8" discs of 60- and 120-grits. They work great on sanding lumber up to almost 2" thick.

I suggest taking your time when you're getting used to this tool—don't set the fence too tightly or too loosely. With some careful experimentation, you'll get the hang for how much wiggle room you need and how fast or slow to feed the stock. The stock should be able to move freely enough so there is no chance of it binding up, but it should not be so loose that it can move from side to side and create a risk of kickback. To increase safety, it's easy to mount featherboards to the rip fence.

Shop IDEAS

1. A wooden block, grooved for a tight press fit over the circular saw fence, is a useful aid when cutting work to length.

2. Covered with garnet paper on both sides, a plywood disk mounted on the saw arbor sands work to exact width.

3. A paper fan on the router bit will keep the work free from shavings.

4. If your work calls for frequent shifting of the drill press head, fit the clamping bolt with a handle. The one shown here is a standard Delta part, No. NCS-361-S, and can be obtained for fifty cents. It requires re-tapping, (½-inch N. C. or U. S. S. screw thread) to fit.

5. When tapping work on the lathe, the tool rest slipped under the chuck will prevent it from turning.

6. A "peep hole" on the auxiliary wood fence used with the moulding head shows the exact position of the cutters.

parts list

NO.	COMPONENT	MATERIAL	THICKNESS X WIDTH X LENGTH	
			INCHES	MILLIMETERS
1	sanding disk blank	plywood	$^1/_2 \times 8^1/_2 \times 8^1/_2$	13 × 305 × 305
1	blank for throat plate	plywood	$^1/_2 \times 4 \times 12$	13 × 102 × 305
1	self-adhesive sanding disc		8 D	203 D

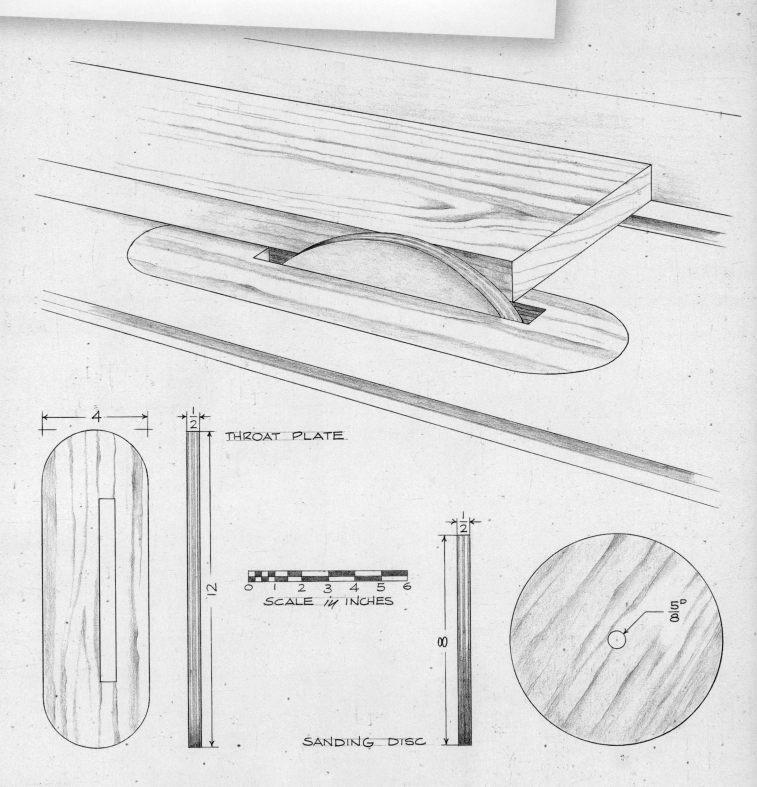

THROAT PLATE

4

$\frac{1}{2}$

12

0 1 2 3 4 5 6

SCALE in INCHES

$\frac{1}{2}$

8

$\frac{5}{8}$D

SANDING DISC

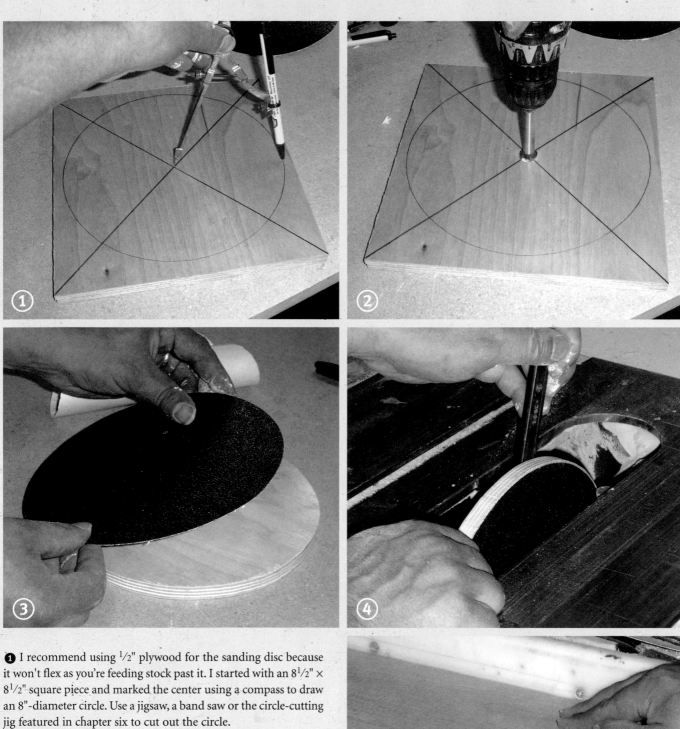

1 I recommend using $1/2$" plywood for the sanding disc because it won't flex as you're feeding stock past it. I started with an $8^1/2$" × $8^1/2$" square piece and marked the center using a compass to draw an 8"-diameter circle. Use a jigsaw, a band saw or the circle-cutting jig featured in chapter six to cut out the circle.

2 Using a $5/8$" Forstner bit, I cut a hole in the center of the disc.

3 The sandpaper has adhesive on the back. After it's attached to the disc, I use the same Forstner bit as before to cut a hole through the sandpaper.

4 Mount the sanding disc on the saw just like an ordinary saw blade.

5 I made a throat plate to accommodate the size of the sanding disc—time well spent for safety's sake.

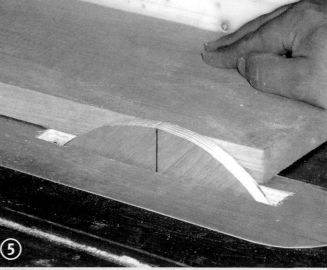

69

THE DELTAGRAM

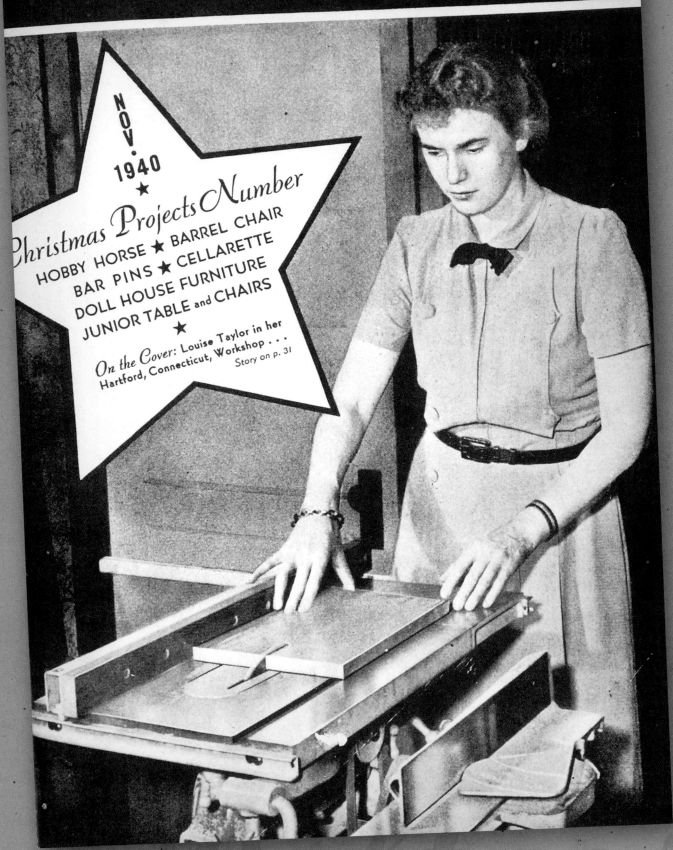

NOV. 1940

★

Christmas Projects Number

HOBBY HORSE ★ BARREL CHAIR
BAR PINS ★ CELLARETTE
DOLL HOUSE FURNITURE
JUNIOR TABLE and CHAIRS

★

On the Cover: Louise Taylor in her
Hartford, Connecticut, Workshop . . .
Story on p. 31

ANCHOR POINT →

①

Shop TIPS

SANDER FENCE

OPENING TO SUIT WORK

1—A board provided with anchor points and fitted with a wood or metal bar to slide in the circular saw table slot is useful in sawing where the work has no smooth edge. In use, the work is pressed down on the anchor points, and then, riding the wood table, is projected into the saw blade. 2—Bottle cap corks placed under the screws of the miter gage clamp attachment will prevent marring of fine veneer panels. 3—Oiled silk or Pliofilm pan covers make ideal dust protectors for buffing wheels. 4—A simple vee-shaped jig used on the belt sander provides one of the neatest and fastest methods for beveling edges of short work. Drawing at right shows the jig with one end removed. The work is simply placed in the jig and held in contact with the sanding belt until the cut is complete. 5—The increasing size of saw tables makes it difficult to lean over the table to observe the mark for sawing. An idea which solves this problem is to use a mirror at the end of the saw table. This should be mounted in some simple manner so that it can be pushed out of the way when not in use.

②

③

④

⑤

BORING DEEP HOLES ON THE DRILL PRESS

I have a small benchtop drill press which works well for my everyday needs, but it occasionally lacks the capacity to perform more challenging operations. When I saw this Deltagram, I realized that I may have been selling it short. With a few modifications, this humble tool could be capable of drilling much deeper holes than I would've imagined. I had no problem drilling a 20"-deep hole that was nicely centered in the workpiece.

The first step was to remove the drill press from its base and screw it to a workbench. This created a deeper space for working and facilitated the use of long drill bits and extensions. If you have a floor-standing drill press, this step probably won't be necessary.

The jig described in the Deltagram provides a stable support post that can be used to hold the workpiece steady so I adapted this idea to my setup. I supported the workpiece from below by using a milk crate and a series of ¾" plywood scraps—as the hole deepens, the workpiece can be moved up and supported by a few more of these makeshift spacers. The dimensions and configurations presented here won't be universally applicable, my workbench might not be the same height as yours, but the concept is the same.

Boring DEEP HOLES

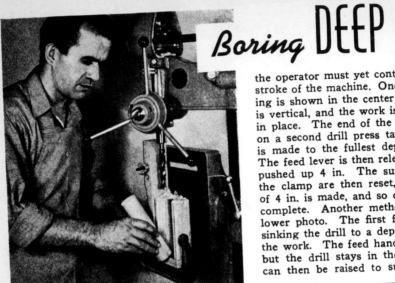

THE stroke of the 14-inch Delta drill press is 4 in., and the standard bit supplied has a twist of 4 in. What happens, then, when you want to bore a hole 7 in. deep—almost twice the length of the fluted portion of the drill?

Perhaps the simplest solution to work of this kind is to drill from both ends. The upper photo is an example. The table is tilted vertical, and the work, a cylinder, is aligned by means of a vee block. The capacity of a 4-in. twist is thus increased to 8 in. In every case where the drilling is done from opposite sides, great care must be exercised in lining up the work. A useful method is shown in the sketch. The required drill is chucked, and a hole is drilled in the auxiliary wood table or in a piece of wood clamped to the table. A length of metal rod or a straight piece of dowel stock is now placed in the chuck, its purpose being to correctly align the hole exactly below the chuck. The final step in the operation is as shown in Fig. 3. The hole is drilled as deeply as possible from one side, then a wood guide pin is placed in the hole in the table and the work is placed over the guide pin. Thus aligned, the second hole meets the first hole for a perfect through shot.

Where a longer twist than 4 in. is being used, the bit may be long enough to go through the work, but

the operator must yet contend with the 4 in. stroke of the machine. One method of working is shown in the center photo. The table is vertical, and the work is clamped securely in place. The end of the work is supported on a second drill press table. The first cut is made to the fullest depth possible—4 in. The feed lever is then released and the work pushed up 4 in. The supporting table and the clamp are then reset, and a second cut of 4 in. is made, and so on until the hole is complete. Another method is shown in the lower photo. The first full stroke is made, sinking the drill to a depth of about 4 in. in the work. The feed handle is then released, but the drill stays in the work. The table can then be raised to support the work in

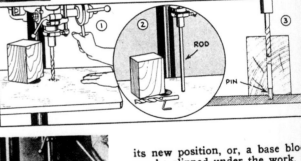

its new position, or, a base block can be slipped under the work, as shown, to give it the required elevation.

In all deep hole drilling, cutting should not continue after the flutes of the bit have passed below the work surface. Where it is absolutely necessary to do this, the bit should be lifted frequently in order to permit clearing the hole of chips.

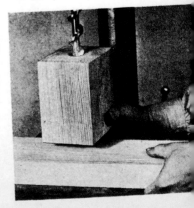

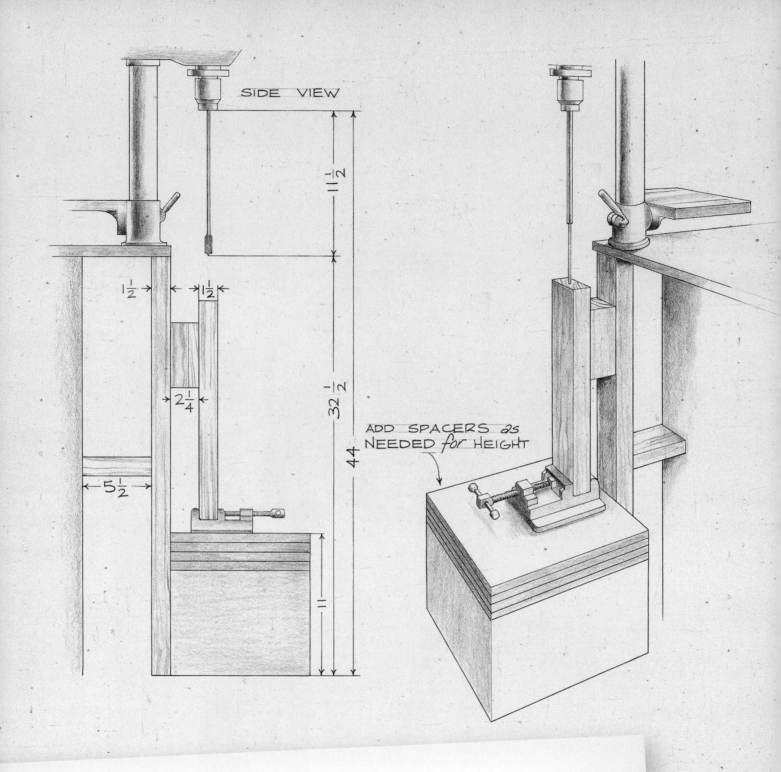

SIDE VIEW

$11\frac{1}{2}$

$1\frac{1}{2}$ $1\frac{1}{2}$

$2\frac{1}{4}$

$32\frac{1}{2}$

44

$5\frac{1}{2}$

11

ADD SPACERS *as* NEEDED *for* HEIGHT

parts list

NO.	COMPONENT	MATERIAL	THICKNESS X WIDTH X LENGTH	
			INCHES	MILLIMETERS
1	vertical support post	2×4	$\frac{1}{2} \times 3\frac{1}{2} \times 32\frac{1}{2}$	13 × 89 × 826
1	brace	2×4	$1\frac{1}{2} \times 3\frac{1}{2} \times 5\frac{1}{2}$	38 × 89 × 140
3	spacers	plywood	$\frac{3}{4} \times 3\frac{1}{2} \times 5$	19 × 89 × 127
1	drill bit		$\frac{1}{2} \times 12$	13 × 305
1	drill bit extender			
10	cutoffs for spacers	plywood	$\frac{3}{4}$	19

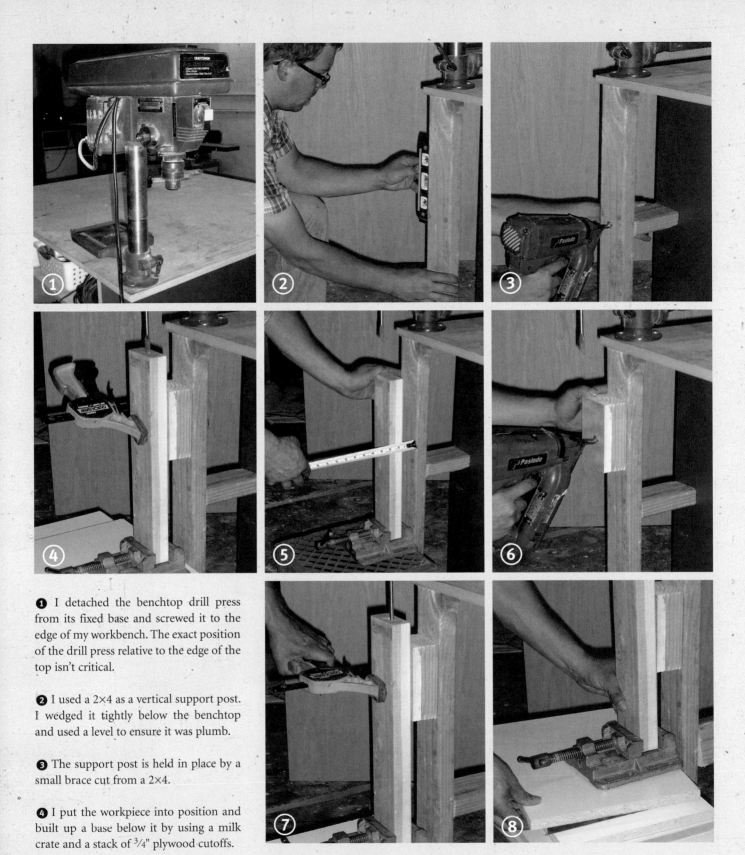

❶ I detached the benchtop drill press from its fixed base and screwed it to the edge of my workbench. The exact position of the drill press relative to the edge of the top isn't critical.

❷ I used a 2×4 as a vertical support post. I wedged it tightly below the benchtop and used a level to ensure it was plumb.

❸ The support post is held in place by a small brace cut from a 2×4.

❹ I put the workpiece into position and built up a base below it by using a milk crate and a stack of ³⁄₄" plywood cutoffs.

❺ There was a 2¹⁄₄" wide gap between the workpiece and the support post. This will be filled with a spacer so that the workpiece can be solidly clamped to the post.

❻ I nailed the spacer into place.

❼ Drilling the hole is almost anticlimactic compared to the time you'll spend on the setup. If you have a benchtop drill press, I would recommend building a separate, floor-standing base for your drill press to accommodate deep boring.

❽ If a deeper hole is needed, you can push the workpiece upward and support it from underneath with more spacers. When you've built it up about 6" or 7", you could substitute a bit extender for the stack of spacers.

DRILLING CENTERED HOLES IN SPHERES

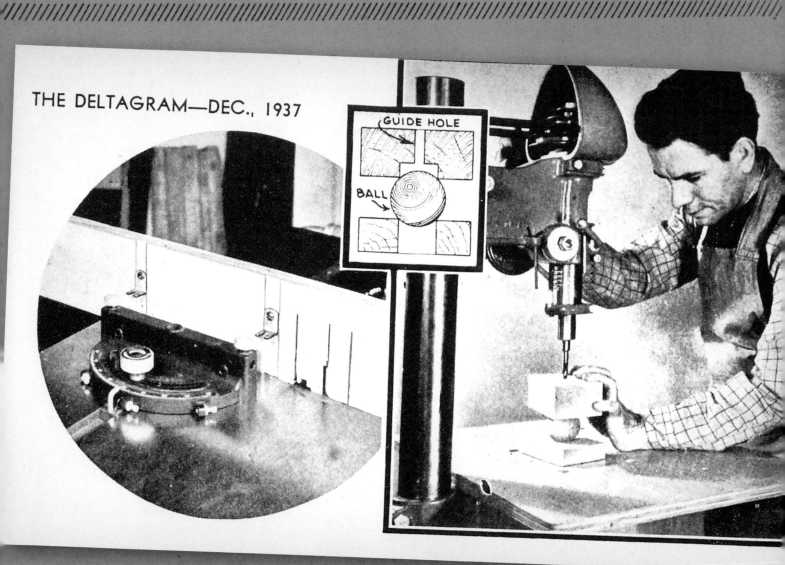

15

THE DELTAGRAM—DEC., 1937

GUIDE HOLE

BALL

Need to drill a hole precisely in the center of a sphere? This jig provides an easy way of doing exactly that. The upper block has a guide hole drilled in the center which is of the same diameter as the drill bit you'll be using. Both blocks are counter-bored on the surfaces which contact the sphere. The exact size of these holes isn't critical, because the sphere will center itself. I used blocks that are ¾" × 4" × 4", and I found that a ¾" Forstner bit worked great for the counterbores.

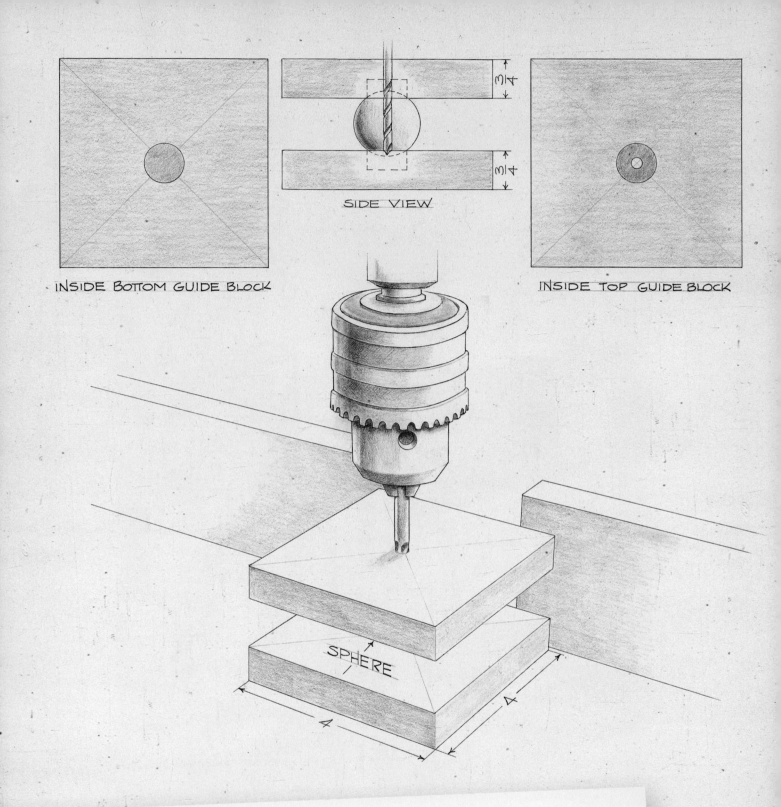

INSIDE BOTTOM GUIDE BLOCK

SIDE VIEW

$\frac{3}{4}$

$\frac{3}{4}$

INSIDE TOP GUIDE BLOCK

SPHERE

4

4

parts list

NO.	COMPONENT	MATERIAL	THICKNESS X WIDTH X LENGTH	
			INCHES	MILLIMETERS
2	guide blocks	MDF	$\frac{3}{4}$ × 4 × 4	19 × 102 × 102

❶ Cut out the guide blocks and mark center holes on both. To do this I drew diagonal lines across the blocks. The intersection of the lines indicates the centers.

❷ Counterbore holes on the inside faces of the guide blocks first.

❸ Use a $^3/_{16}$"-diameter bit to drill the center hole in the top block.

❹ To operate the jig, place the sphere between the guide blocks. The sphere will automatically position itself in the center of the counterbored holes, and consequently, on the center hole in the upper block. I didn't find it necessary to clamp or secure the assembly, but if you'd like, you could use masking tape as shown on page 76.

tip

If you wanted to get fancy, you could attach the two guides together using four slotted metal or wooden strips with screws. For different sized spheres, loosen the screws, insert the sphere and tighten the screws. The strips and screws will hold the guide blocks in proper alignment.

DRILL BIT CADDY

16

The original Delta-gram describes a clever but very elaborate solution for storing drill bits. I would imagine that it might have seemed pretty handy at the time. However in this day and age it is hard to believe that anyone would really take the time to build such a complex container when similar things are available at any hardware store for just a couple of dollars. So I decided to take the concept to a different level and design something that is simpler but at the same time even more useful. The resulting caddy is an attempt to effectively store not only drill bits, but the whole gamut of related accessories that are now standard issue in most shops. I used a drill bit organizer that required a 2½" × 9" × 13" space. You'll want to adjust the dimensions to suit your own needs.

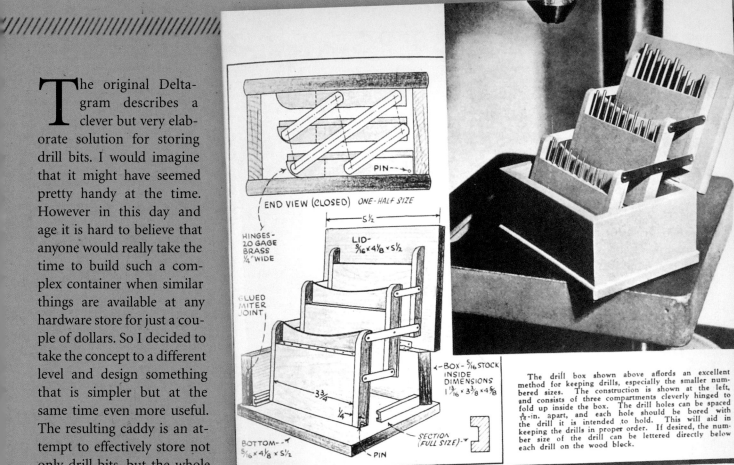

END VIEW (CLOSED) *ONE-HALF SIZE*

HINGES - 20 GAGE BRASS ¼" WIDE

GLUED MITER JOINT

PIN

LID - 5/16 × 4⅛ × 5½

5½

3¾

¼

BOX - 5/16 STOCK INSIDE DIMENSIONS 1 13/16 × 3⅜ × 4⅝

BOTTOM - 5/16 × 4⅛ × 5½

PIN

SECTION (FULL SIZE)

The drill box shown above affords an excellent method for keeping drills, especially the smaller numbered sizes. The construction is shown at the left, and consists of three compartments cleverly hinged to fold up inside the box. The drill holes can be spaced 7/16-in. apart, and each hole should be bored with the drill it is intended to hold. This will aid in keeping the drills in proper order. If desired, the number size of the drill can be lettered directly below each drill on the wood block.

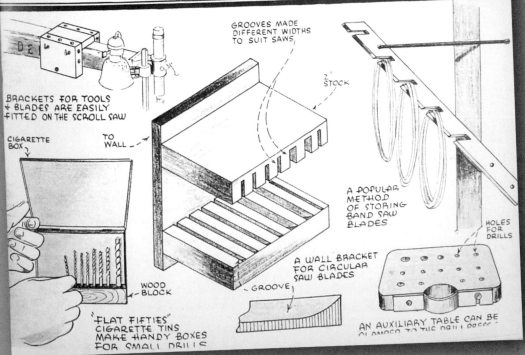

BRACKETS FOR TOOLS + BLADES ARE EASILY FITTED ON THE SCROLL SAW

CIGARETTE BOX

TO WALL

GROOVES MADE DIFFERENT WIDTHS TO SUIT SAWS

½ STOCK

A POPULAR METHOD OF STORING BAND SAW BLADES

A WALL BRACKET FOR CIRCULAR SAW BLADES

HOLES FOR DRILLS

WOOD BLOCK

GROOVE

"FLAT FIFTIES" CIGARETTE TINS MAKE HANDY BOXES FOR SMALL DRILLS

AN AUXILIARY TABLE CAN BE CLAMPED TO THE DRILL PRESS

parts list

NO.	COMPONENT	MATERIAL	THICKNESS X WIDTH X LENGTH INCHES	THICKNESS X WIDTH X LENGTH MILLIMETERS
2	sides	Baltic birch	$1/2 \times 5 \times 15^{1}/2$	$13 \times 127 \times 394$
1	top	Baltic birch	$1/2 \times 5 \times 9$	$13 \times 127 \times 229$
1	bottom	Baltic birch	$1/2 \times 5 \times 9$	$13 \times 127 \times 229$
2	fixed shelves	Baltic birch	$1/2 \times 2^{1}/4 \times 9$	$13 \times 57 \times 229$
1	back	Baltic birch	$1/2 \times 9 \times 14^{1}/2$	$13 \times 229 \times 368$
1	door	veneered plywood	$3/4 \times 10 \times 15^{1}/2$	$19 \times 254 \times 394$
1	pair of hinges			

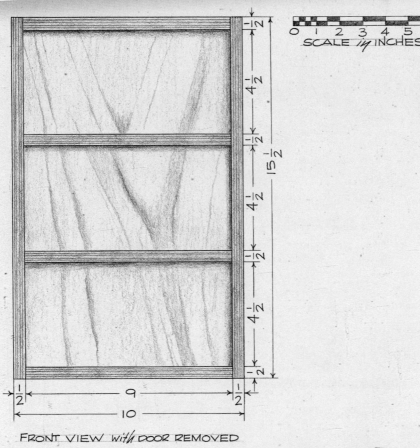

SCALE in INCHES

FRONT VIEW with DOOR REMOVED

SIDE VIEW

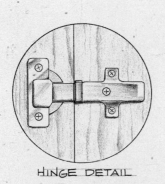

HINGE DETAIL

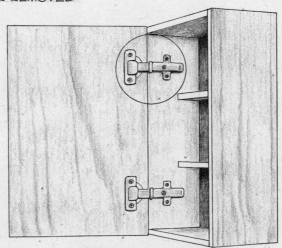

① Once you've inventoried the objects that you want to store, figure out the necessary dimensions for the organizer. The basis of the organizer, regardless of size, is a box that will hang on the wall like a cabinet. I used ¹⁄₂" Baltic birch plywood for all five sides of the box. Use whatever construction materials suit your fancy.

② A couple of fixed shelves will help make the most of the interior.

③ The door is made of plywood so the store-bought organizer can be screwed to it. If you'd like to dress it up a bit, you could build a frame-and-panel door.

④ Hang the door using 35mm European hinges or butt hinges.

17

MAKING DOWELS ON THE SHAPER

You can buy dowels in a number of different species and diameters, but in case you ever need an odd size or species, this method is very effective. You can also save some money by doing it yourself, since hardwood dowels, especially in the larger diameters, can be expensive.

I don't have a shaper, so I used a 3 horsepower router mounted in a router table with great results. I began with 1" square blanks and a 1/2" roundover bit. Different sized router bits will allow you to create dowels of various diameters. After tinkering with the bit height and the fence for a few minutes, I was able to produce perfect 1"-diameter dowels that required no sanding. I don't think I'll ever need to buy dowels again.

MAKING DOWELS on the SHAPER

PERFECT dowels, especially the larger sizes, can be made by using various cutters on the shaper. The largest size which can be made is 1 in. diameter, this being done with D-103 cutter in the manner shown. Four cuts are necessary, one on each corner, to reduce the square stock to cylindrical form. The finished work is much superior to ordinary lathe work, and the operation is done in a fraction of the time. Other sizes which can be made with the four-cut method comprise 1/4, 5/8, and 3/4-in. The size will naturally dictate which of the various cutters to use. With this method, the 3/4 and 1-in. sizes are the most practical.

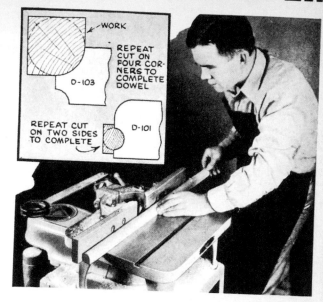

Smaller dowels are best made with the second method shown in the sketch. This requires but two cuts, one on either side of the stock, to complete the full dowel shape. D-102 cutter produces a dowel 1/4 in. in diameter, while D-101 cutter makes a dowel 3/8 in. in diameter.

Either method demands a little care in setting the cutter to the right depth and aligning the fence. After the set-up has been made, a stock quantity can be run off in jig time at a considerable savings over the commercial price for dowel rod, which is usually quite high.

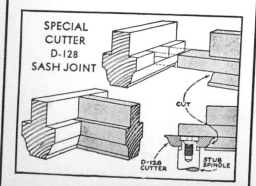

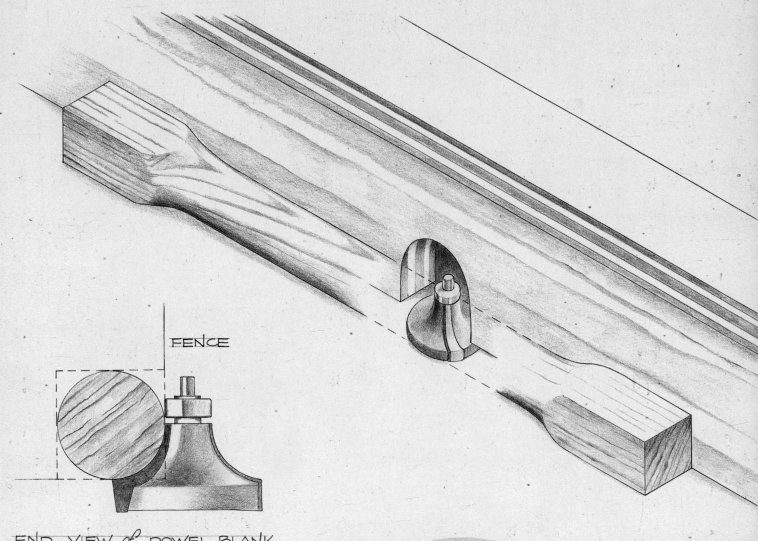

FENCE

END VIEW of DOWEL BLANK

safety tip

When making larger diameter dowels, you may want to use a stop block to hold the blank steady when starting the cut. Clamp a block on the infeed end of your router table fence, rest the end of the blank against the block and push the blank into the router bit to start the cut.

❶ Begin the process with a square blank. I recommend making a couple of extra blanks to use while you are fine-tuning the router settings. Make the blanks about 6" longer than finished length.

❷ You'll need to use a fence on the router table—a piloted bit by itself won't adequately support the workpiece. The fence should be set even with the outer edge of the bearing.

❸ When routing, don't go from end to end on the workpiece—leave a couple of inches at the front and back of the blanks. This will provide a flat, consistent surface for the blank to ride on and will keep the blank at the correct height as it is being advanced past the cutter.

❹ You can cut off the excess on a miter saw.

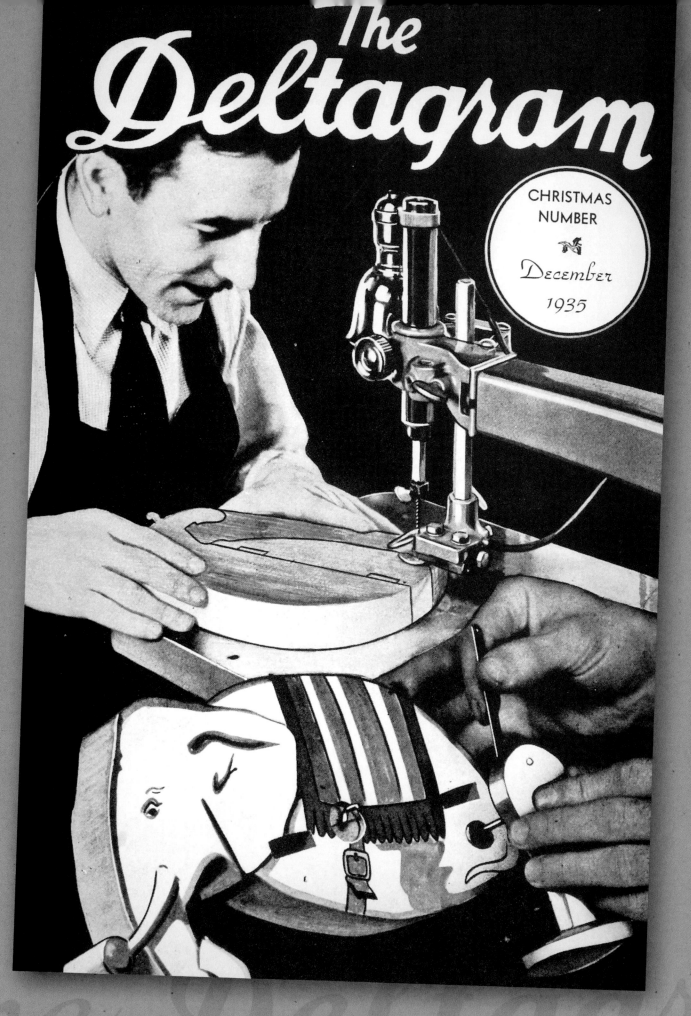

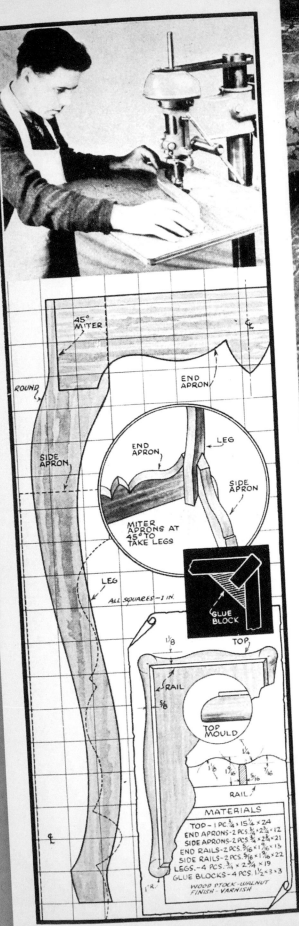

MATERIALS

TOP - 1 PC. ¾ × 15¾ × 24
END APRONS - 2 PCS. ¾ × 2¾ × 12
SIDE APRONS - 2 PCS. ¾ × 2¾ × 21
END RAILS - 2 PCS. ⁵⁄₁₆ × 1⁷⁄₁₆ × 13
SIDE RAILS - 2 PCS. ⁵⁄₁₆ × 1⁷⁄₁₆ × 22
LEGS - 4 PCS. ¾ × 2¾ × 19
GLUE BLOCKS - 4 PCS. 1½ × 3 × 3

WOOD STOCK - WALNUT
FINISH - VARNISH

COFFEE TABLE

VERY simple in design and construction, this table is nevertheless quite attractive in walnut with a bright finish. The tray portion is fixed directly to the table top, but a removable tray with glass bottom could be readily substituted.

Start the construction by glueing up stock for the top, and while this is setting-up, complete the legs, aprons and rails to the dimensions indicated in the drawing. The curved bottom of the rails can be varied in design, or a plain apron with moulded edge can be used. There is a slight round to the outer edge of the legs, which can be run in on the drill press, as shown in the upper photo. The assembly of aprons and legs is made with dowels and glue blocks, the ends of the aprons being mitered so that the legs will set diagonally in each corner.

The top can now be band sawed to size, and a suitable moulding run in around the edge, using either the drill press or shaper. The top surface of the top is sanded smooth, and the tray rails are fitted in place, being held by screws inserted from the underside of the top. The top, in turn, is held to the table framework by means of screws countersunk from the underside of the aprons.

18

CUTTING TENONS ON THE JOINTER

The jointer is capable of a lot more than simply putting a straight edge on boards. However, cutting tenons requires you to remove the blade guard, so be extremely careful. Don't operate this tool without a guard during normal circumstances.

I suggest using a fairly wide stop-block (5" in this case), because a wider block is more stable when it is positioned against the fence.

Unusual JOINTER OPERATIONS

MOST craftsmen use the jointer for surfacing and edge jointing only, seldom taking advantage of this machine for tapering, cutting tenons, making mouldings, and the many other jobs which can be done with the jointer.

One of the most useful of these lesser-used methods is the making of shaped edges. Fig. 2 shows a wide variety of such work, all done on the jointer. The various cove moulds may puzzle some workers until reference is made to Fig. 1. It can be seen in this picture that coves of various sizes can be readily cut by running the work more or less parallel with the knives against an auxiliary fence. Other cuts, such as bevels and shoulders, are made with the use of the standard tilting fence and by rabbeting.

Fig. 3 shows an operation which is useful in making building trim. Practically all trim is relieved on the back side with a wide shallow groove so that it will hang snug to the plaster. One of the simplest ways of machining this groove is by the jointer method shown, running the work over the knives at an angle to cut the width groove required. With the 6 in. jointer, grooves from 3 to 6 in. wide can be cut, while the 4 in. unit will cut grooves from 2 to 4 in. wide. The depth of cut should be about ⅛ in. Where deeper cuts than this must be made, it is advisable to make the cut in two or three passes of the work. It can be seen that any cut the full width of the jointer knife is "heavy going." Where much cutting of this nature must be done, it is advisable to fit the jointer with a holddown so that the work will be firmly pressed against the knives.

Fig. 4 shows the jointer method of making a tenon on the end of round stock. This is the best and fastest method of doing this particular job. A simple wood block guides the work and sets the length of the tenon. The jointer table is set to the required depth. Work to be tenoned is placed against the block and pushed into the revolving cutter. After coming to rest on the stop shoulder, the work is slowly rotated, turning in the same direction as cutterhead.

Above, Cutting a Cove Moulding on the Jointer.

MOULDINGS CUT ON JOINTER (No Scale)

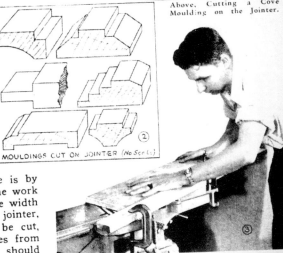

Examples of Moulded Work, and, Below, Cutting Tenons on the Jointer.

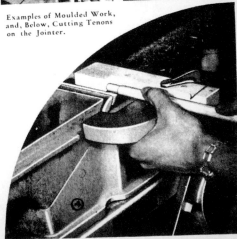

TENON

parts list

NO.	COMPONENT	MATERIAL	THICKNESS X WIDTH X LENGTH		COMMENTS
			INCHES	MILLIMETERS	
1	stop	MDF	$3/4 \times 12 \times 14$	$19 \times 305 \times 356$	Cut to fit your jointer.
1	hold down	hardwood	$7/8 \times 1^{1}/2 \times 7$	$22 \times 38 \times 178$	

1 I used my band saw to cut out the L-shaped base plate. Make it large enough to clamp the plate in two places.

2 A hardwood strip serves as both a hold down for the dowel and a guard to cover the jointer knives. Cut the hold down as shown.

3 Pre-drill the hole in the strip. Then set the dowel in place, locate the hold down on the base plate and attach the hold down with a screw.

4 When using the jig, feed the dowel into the jointer knives, rotating it clockwise. The result is a smooth and symmetrical tenon that is safe to do using the jointer.

safety tip

Once the base plate is in place, the depth of cut can be adjusted by raising or lowering the infeed table. For safety's sake, remove a small amount of stock with each pass. This will also allow you to fine tune the final diameter of the tenon.

19

SPLITTING DOWELS ON THE BAND SAW

I build a lot of projects that get finished off with a variety of different mouldings and I occasionally need some half-round trim for this purpose. This is a rather unusual profile and it is difficult to find in more than one or two species of wood, so I usually end up making my own. This jig provides a very effective way of doing so. You can even use this jig as a follow-up to chapter seventeen (Making Dowels on the Shaper) and you won't even need to leave your shop for a trip to the home center.

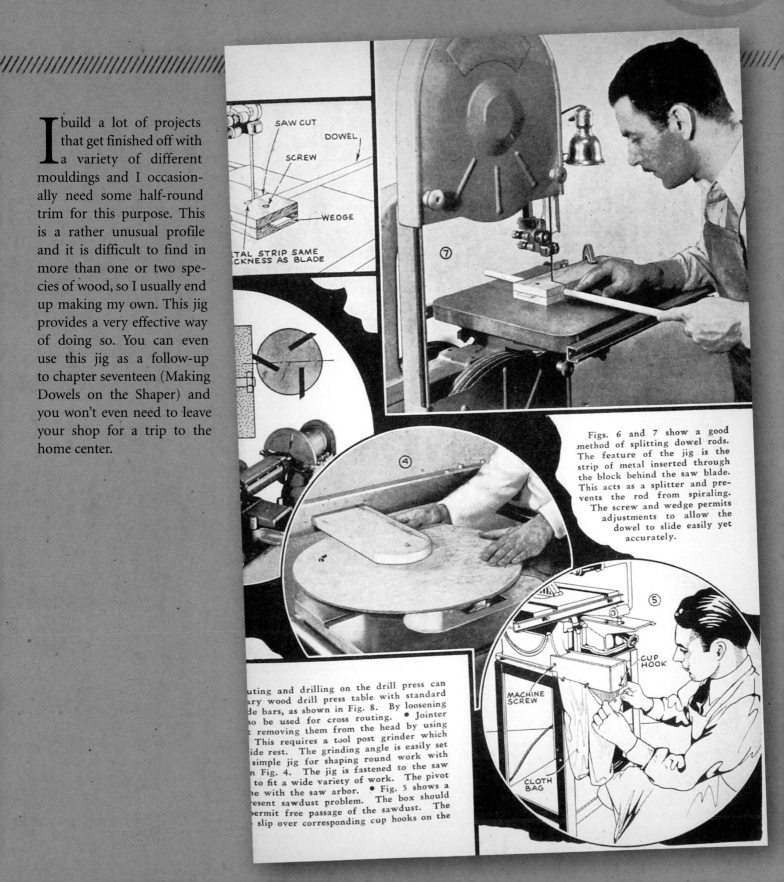

Figs. 6 and 7 show a good method of splitting dowel rods. The feature of the jig is the strip of metal inserted through the block behind the saw blade. This acts as a splitter and prevents the rod from spiraling. The screw and wedge permits adjustments to allow the dowel to slide easily yet accurately.

uting and drilling on the drill press can ary wood drill press table with standard de bars, as shown in Fig. 8. By loosening so be used for cross routing. • Jointer removing them from the head by using This requires a tool post grinder which ide rest. The grinding angle is easily set simple jig for shaping round work with n Fig. 4. The jig is fastened to the saw to fit a wide variety of work. The pivot he with the saw arbor. • Fig. 5 shows a resent sawdust problem. The box should ermit free passage of the sawdust. The slip over corresponding cup hooks on the

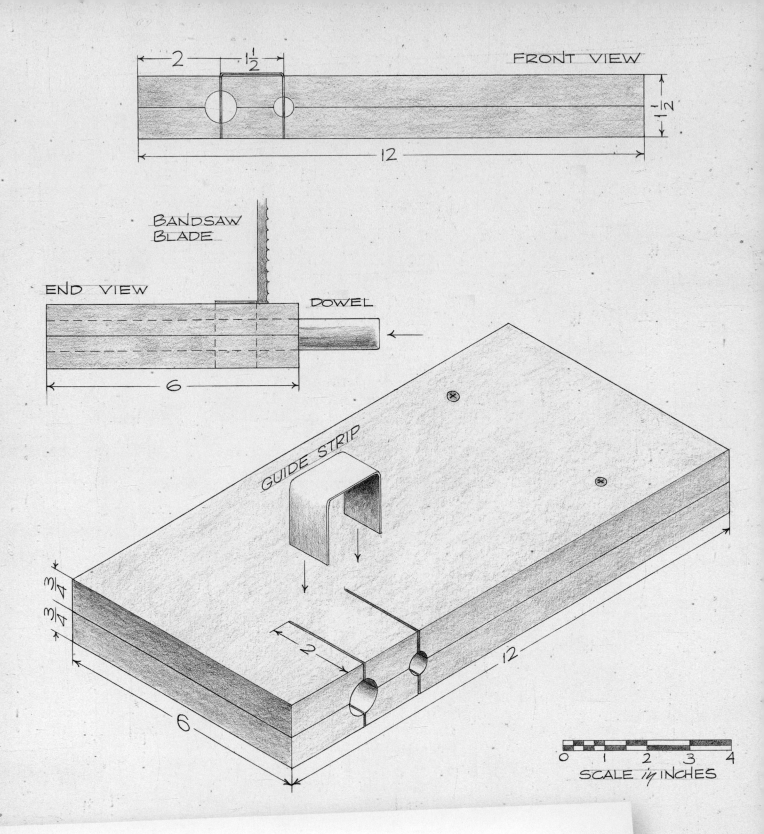

FRONT VIEW

2
1½
12
1½

BANDSAW BLADE

END VIEW

DOWEL

6

GUIDE STRIP

2

12

6

¾

¾

0 1 2 3 4

SCALE in INCHES

parts list

NO.	COMPONENT	MATERIAL	THICKNESS X WIDTH X LENGTH	
			INCHES	MILLIMETERS
1	guide block	MDF	¾ × 12 × 12	19 × 305 × 305
1	splitter	scrap tin	1¼ × 5	32 × 127

❶ Using a core box bit in conjunction with a router table, rout a couple of grooves near the end of the block. I suggest using a few differently-sized bits, if you have them, since you may find they'll help you to accommodate a larger range of dowels.

❷ Cut the block into two identical halves.

❸ The halves get stacked on top of each other with the grooves aligned on the inside faces.

❹ Drill a pilot hole through the top block and screw the two halves together.

❺ Use a square to draw lines 2" long down the center of each channel.

❻ Cut along the lines.

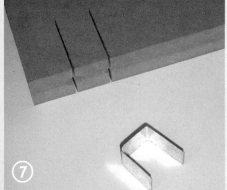

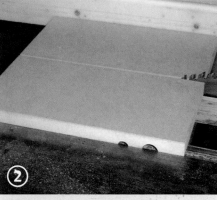

❼ Fit the fixture with a guide strip to keep the dowel aligned and prevent it from spiraling while it's being cut. Because I created two channels to accommodate dowels of various sizes, I fashioned a U-shaped piece of tin which I inserted from the top of the fixture—this takes care of both channels at once.

❽ Clamp the fixture to the band saw's table. Back the band saw blade into the kerf while the saw is turned off. The dowel can then be placed inside the groove that fits best—an exact fit is not required. Just tighten the screw to achieve a snug but not overly tight fit.

20

PATTERN SAWING ON THE TABLE SAW

If you need to make a number of identical curved parts, this setup might be the ticket. I like to use MDF for the patterns because it is easy to work with and I usually have some scraps on hand.

This method of using the table saw is highly unusual, but it is quite safe as long as you take precautions to avoid kickback. The important thing is to trim the workpiece fairly close to the pattern prior to turning on the saw: I suggest having no more than 1/4" of material exposed beyond the edge of the pattern. With this technique, you're basically just nibbling away at the excess rather than cutting off large overhanging pieces.

This process is especially suited to convex curves.

PATTERN SAWING
In Production Work

PATTERN SAWING on the circular saw can be used to good advantage in production work in cutting any shape comprised of straight lines, such as shown in Fig. 1. It is extremely fast, and has the great advantage that short pieces of waste stock can be quickly worked to size.

The general set-up is shown in Fig. 2. There is an auxiliary wood fence, which

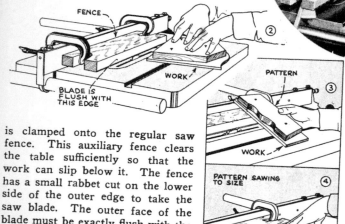

FENCE

BLADE IS FLUSH WITH THIS EDGE

WORK

PATTERN

WORK

PATTERN SAWING TO SIZE

SHAPING THE CURVED EDGE

is clamped onto the regular saw fence. This auxiliary fence clears the table sufficiently so that the work can slip below it. The fence has a small rabbet cut on the lower side of the outer edge to take the saw blade. The outer face of the blade must be exactly flush with the outer face of the fence. A pattern cut to the shape desired is necessary. This is fitted with any style of anchor point (nails or phonograph needles are the simplest) so that it can be temporarily fastened to the work, as shown in Fig. 2. After the pattern is fastened to the work, it is a simple matter to guide each edge of the pattern along the fence, and thus cut the work to the same exact shape as the pattern.

A typical set-up is shown in Figs. 3, 4, and 5. Fig. 3 shows the pattern fastened to the work. Fig. 4 shows the work being pattern sawed. Fig. 5 shows how the curved portion of the work can now be completely cut with the shaper. It can be seen that any piece of work can be cut to shape in this manner, and then, using the same pattern, it can be taken to the shaper and moulded with any selected cutter by riding the pattern against the shaper collar.

Fig. 6 shows another common application of pattern sawing. In this particular case, no pattern is necessary since the work itself is the pattern. The job is to cut off the cleats flush with the edges of the work.

The cutting is done easily and quickly by simply running each edge of the work in turn along the fence. The same general method applies to trimming veneer edges flush with the main body of wood to which it is applied.

Try this method the next time you have a number of straight-line pieces to get out. When the stock being worked is plywood, pattern sawing offers a perfect method of utilizing odd-shaped scraps, which would be by any other method, difficult to line up properly with either the standard fence or miter gage.

When fire cabinet woods are worked by this method, it is sometimes undesirable to use anchor points. In this case it is usually a simple matter to make some kind of frame around the pattern to hold the work. This is very seldom necessary, however, since the very fine indentation made by phonograph needle anchor points is practically invisible, and easily filled in with paste filler.

parts list

NO.	COMPONENT	MATERIAL	THICKNESS X WIDTH X LENGTH		COMMENTS
			INCHES	MILLIMETERS	
1	pattern	MDF	$3/4 \times 6 \times 12$	$19 \times 152 \times 305$	The pattern and workpiece dimensions
					represent the sample project,
1	workpiece	MDF	$1/4 \times 6^1/2 \times 12$	$6 \times 165 \times 305$	but this technique will work with parts
					of many different sizes.
1	auxiliary fence	hardwood	$3/4 \times 2 \times 30$	$19 \times 51 \times 762$	
2	shims	MDF	$1/4 \times 2 \times 2$	$6 \times 51 \times 51$	
	double-stick tape				

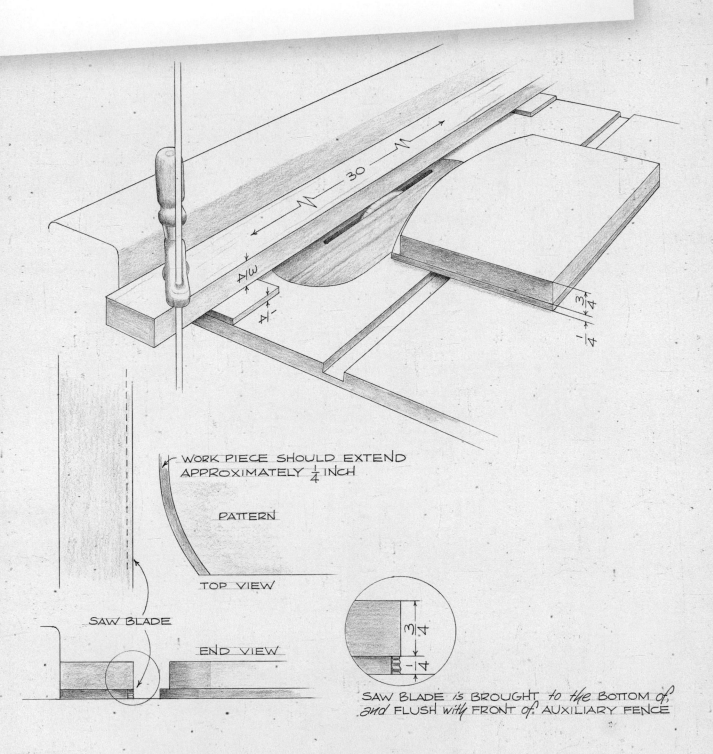

WORK PIECE SHOULD EXTEND APPROXIMATELY $\frac{1}{4}$ INCH

PATTERN

TOP VIEW

SAW BLADE

END VIEW

SAW BLADE IS BROUGHT to the BOTTOM of and FLUSH with FRONT of AUXILIARY FENCE

1 Make a full-size pattern for the part you'll be fabricating. I use MDF for pattern.

2 Rough-out a blank that is just slightly larger than the pattern. Align the back edges of the pattern and template and trace the front edge of the pattern.

3 Using a jigsaw or a band saw, cut out the blank and make sure to cut about ¼" outside the line. This cut doesn't need to be precise, so some variation is nothing to worry about. The workpiece can be secured to the pattern with double-stick tape.

4 This process requires a guide fence that is shimmed up with some scrap stock that is of the same thickness as your workpiece. The guide fence could also be clamped to the table saw's fence. The edge of the blade should be set flush with the outside edge of the fence.

5 When you're ready to roll, nibble away the excess on the front edge of the workpiece by passing it from front to back across the saw blade. The pattern will hug the edge of the guide fence and the blade will do its work quickly. The finished result should require very little sanding.

WALL CABINET

21

Making good use of wall space to store tools and supplies is nothing new—woodworkers have been building cabinets of this style for at least a couple of hundred years. Some are extremely elaborate and others are more modest. Not surprisingly, most designs seem to reflect the unique personalities and work habits of the people who create them. In my case, I like to have my frequently used measuring and layout tools clearly and conveniently displayed, so I allotted them a premium position inside one of the doors.

I decided to use pegboard for part of the interior because I wanted to make sure the cabinet offered methods of storage that could be easily rearranged to accommodate some inevitable new tool purchases.

This cabinet is definitely a product of a modern era: I included a power strip to provide a central place to plug in the battery chargers for my cordless tools. This also turned out to be a great place to plug in my iPod and speakers.

Because clutter drives me crazy, I enjoy being able to close the doors and instantly neaten up the workshop. I painted the doors in some fun, bold colors and decided to display my business logo for a professional touch.

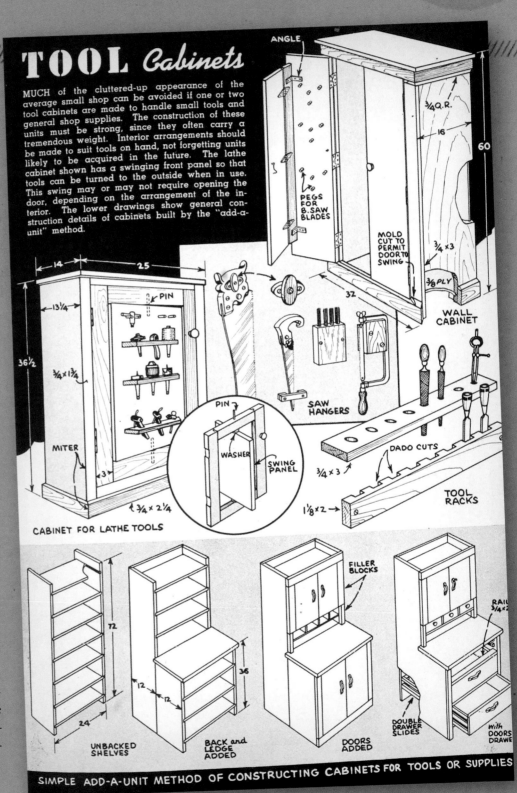

TOOL Cabinets

MUCH of the cluttered-up appearance of the average small shop can be avoided if one or two tool cabinets are made to handle small tools and general shop supplies. The construction of these units must be strong, since they often carry a tremendous weight. Interior arrangements should be made to suit tools on hand, not forgetting units likely to be acquired in the future. The lathe cabinet shown has a swinging front panel so that tools can be turned to the outside when in use. This swing may or may not require opening the door, depending on the arrangement of the interior. The lower drawings show general construction details of cabinets built by the "add-a-unit" method.

CABINET FOR LATHE TOOLS

WALL CABINET

SAW HANGERS

DADO CUTS

TOOL RACKS

PEGS FOR B. SAW BLADES

MOLD CUT TO PERMIT DOOR TO SWING

SWING PANEL

WASHER

PIN

UNBACKED SHELVES

BACK and LEDGE ADDED

DOORS ADDED

FILLER BLOCKS

DOUBLE DRAWER SLIDES

with DOORS DRAWE

RAIL 3/4 x 2

SIMPLE ADD-A-UNIT METHOD OF CONSTRUCTING CABINETS FOR TOOLS OR SUPPLIES

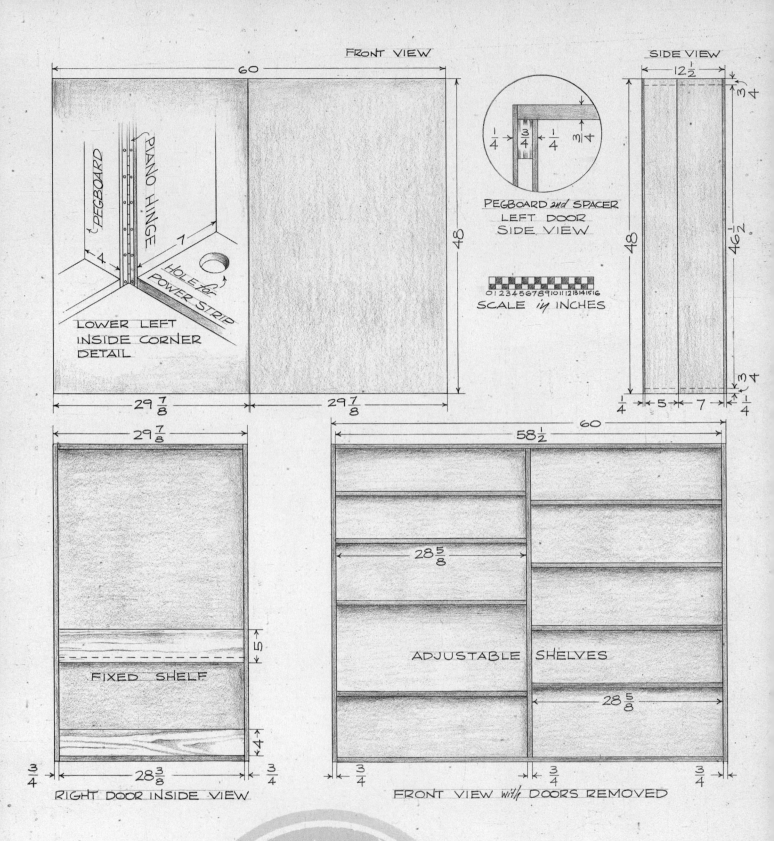

FRONT VIEW

60

48

PEGBOARD

PIANO HINGE

4

1

HOLE for POWER STRIP

LOWER LEFT
INSIDE CORNER
DETAIL

29 7/8

29 7/8

SIDE VIEW

12 1/2

3/4

48

46 1/2

3/4

1/4   5   7   1/4

PEGBOARD and SPACER
LEFT DOOR
SIDE VIEW

1/4   3/4   1/4   3/4

0 1 2 3 4 5 6 7 8 9 10 11 12 13 14 15 16

SCALE in INCHES

29 7/8

58 1/2

60

5

FIXED SHELF

4 1/4

3/4   28 3/8   3/4

RIGHT DOOR INSIDE VIEW

28 5/8

ADJUSTABLE   SHELVES

28 5/8

3/4   3/4   3/4

FRONT VIEW with DOORS REMOVED

tip

When you're deciding on the size of your cabinet, go ahead and physically lay out your tools just like you want them stored in the cabinet. Then take your measurements. Also, make the cabinet with an extra shelf or compartment for those tools you'll be acquiring in the future.

❶ The cabinet can be built to whatever size you like. I took a bigger-is-better approach—I had a nice open space on one wall and decided to fill up most of it. This established the dimensions: 60" × 48". I began the construction by cutting out the back. I used a circular saw to cut out this panel since it was too big for my table saw. I cleaned up the edges with a power planer. I like white melamine for the cabinet back because it brightens the interior.

❷ I measured some of my tools and accessories and determined that I'd need 7" of depth inside the cabinet. I cut out the sides, top and bottom of the cabinet and joined them with screws set into counterbored holes. I edge-banded the particleboard edges and drilled the holes for the shelf pegs prior to assembling the cabinet.

❸ You can't overdo it when it comes to securing the back to the cabinet. I used a ton of screws and Roo-Glue, which is an adhesive specifically designed to bond melamine-coated surfaces.

❹ I decided to reinforce the cabinet by supporting it with a pair of metal shelf brackets. This also made the installation a bit easier.

parts list

NO.	COMPONENT	MATERIAL	THICKNESS X WIDTH X LENGTH	
			INCHES	MILLIMETERS
1	cabinet back	melamine	$1/4 \times 48 \times 60$	$6 \times 1219 \times 1524$
2	cabinet sides	plywood or melamine	$3/4 \times 7 \times 48$	$19 \times 178 \times 1219$
1	cabinet top	plywood or melamine	$3/4 \times 7 \times 58^{1}/_{2}$	$19 \times 178 \times 1486$
1	cabinet bottom	plywood or melamine	$3/4 \times 7 \times 58^{1}/_{2}$	$19 \times 178 \times 1486$
4	door box sides	veneered plywood	$3/4 \times 5 \times 48$	$19 \times 127 \times 1219$
4	door box tops/bottoms	veneered plywood	$3/4 \times 5 \times 28^{3}/_{8}$	$19 \times 127 \times 721$
2	door panels	MDF	$1/4 \times 29^{7}/_{8} \times 48$	$6 \times 759 \times 1219$
1	vertical divider	melamine	$3/4 \times 7 \times 46^{1}/_{2}$	$19 \times 178 \times 1181$
8	adjustable shelves	melamine	$3/4 \times 7 \times 28^{5}/_{8}$	$19 \times 178 \times 727$
1	pegboard	hardboard	$1/4 \times 28^{5}/_{8} \times 46^{3}/_{8}$	$6 \times 727 \times 1178$
2	pegboard spacers	plywood	$3/4 \times 2 \times 28$	$19 \times 51 \times 711$

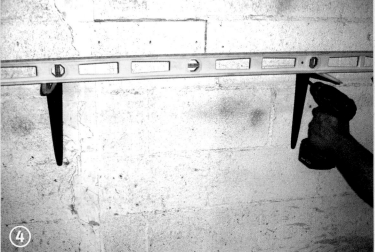

5 Because I work alone, I've learned to plan ahead and I decided to mount the cabinet while it was still a basic lightweight box. A masonry drill bit and Tapcon concrete fasteners provide plenty of support.

6 I used a hole saw to bore the hole for the power strip's cord.

7 To build the interior of the cabinet, I installed a vertical divider that was drilled wih the same peg-hole pattern as the sides. Adjustable shelves are nice because they allow you flexibility.

8 The doors are rectangles which are assembled with screws and glue.

9 To hang the doors, I suggest that you secure the hinges to the cabinet first, then hold the door up at the correct height and run a hinge screw into it. Begin at the top of the door. Once you have one screw in place, things get a lot easier and you can take your time lining up the door. When you're satisfied that the door is straight, you can install the rest of the hinge screws.

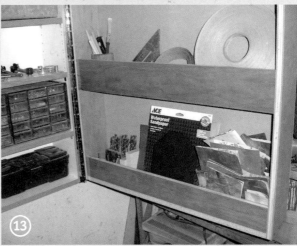

10 I applied the $1/4"$ door panel afterwards—this was a simple way to make sure that the doors were correctly aligned to the cabinet and to each other.

11 The pegboard needs to be installed at least $1/2"$ away from the inside of the door, so I installed a set of plywood strips to act as spacers.

12 Pegboard offers a number of advantages: it's easy to cut and install and it's inexpensive. Several types of holders are available that allow you total flexibility in configuring your tools .

13 In the other door I installed fixed shelves with 4" lips to be sure the shelves keep their contents in place.

The DELTAGRAM

A Magazine for Craftsmen

December 1941

TELEPHONE SET

★ CEDAR CHESTS ★ END TABLE ★

A Young LADY Gets Her First DESK

Cover Photo . . . is none other than Jim Jordan, famous from coast to coast as Fibber McGee of the NBC Red Network. Fibber thinks his Delta saw is tops . . . almost as good as Johnson's Glo-Coat.

"Dishing" on the CIRCULAR SAW

ONE of the lesser known but still useful operations which can be done with the moulding head on the circular saw is the recessing or "dishing" of the work ordinarily done on the lathe. The principle involved is quite simple—the work being pivoted over the center of the cutter and revolved. Thus, the full sweep of the cutter is made in the work, and, by rotating the work, the complete dish-shape is effected. In operation, the saw table is raised to clear the cutter at the beginning of the cut and is then lowered until the knife is cutting to full depth. From this full depth position, the work is revolved to complete the shape. The resulting surface is quite smooth and requires only a minimum amount of sanding.

The example shown was cut with a B-style knife, and is the maximum cut which can be made with standard knives. However, special long knives or different-diameter heads could be used to secure other sizes. Also, with flat knives, the cut can be made with a curve at the outer edges only, running to a flat in the center, a useful form of turned recess.

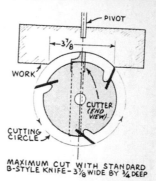

MAXIMUM CUT WITH STANDARD
B-STYLE KNIFE—3⅛ WIDE BY ¾ DEEP

New Steel Moulding-Cutter Head
for Heavy-Duty Work

Hundreds of thousands of feet of mouldings have been made in all kinds of shops by the original Delta moulding cutter. Since so many Delta circular saws are used by industrial and commercial shops there has been an increasing demand for a type of cutter head adaptable for heavier cuts than those for which the original cutter was designed. The new Delta steel cutter head—using the same inexpensive high-speed steel cutter blades as before—is the answer and is now ready for use.

Available for all Delta Circular Saw Units. See the New 1939 Catalog for Description of Knives and Heads in Complete Sets.

Rubber Feet for STEEL STANDS

These feet for steel stands and bench legs will make your machines run smoother and quieter, an advantage where noise must be kept to the minimum. They are of the correct composition to stand hard usage, while having enough flexibility to absorb slight vibrations. Supplied with metal plates to fit in the recesses of our stand feet, and drilled and tapped for machine screws inserted from the top of the feet. Order by catalog number 353. The set of four feet, with plates and screws is priced at

MOBILE CLAMP RACK

22

This rack provides the ideal clamp storage that I have wanted for a long time. The A-shaped frame securely holds about 25 pipe clamps that range in length from 3' to 5' and it also has room for an assortment of smaller clamps. I utilized the space in the interior of the rack by filling it with a bank of drawers. This provides a convenient place to store adhesives, biscuits and other accessories. This rack occupies a 30" × 30" footprint, which fits perfectly into my shop, but you could easily change the size as your needs dictate. A set of open shelves would be a useful substitute for the drawer bank.

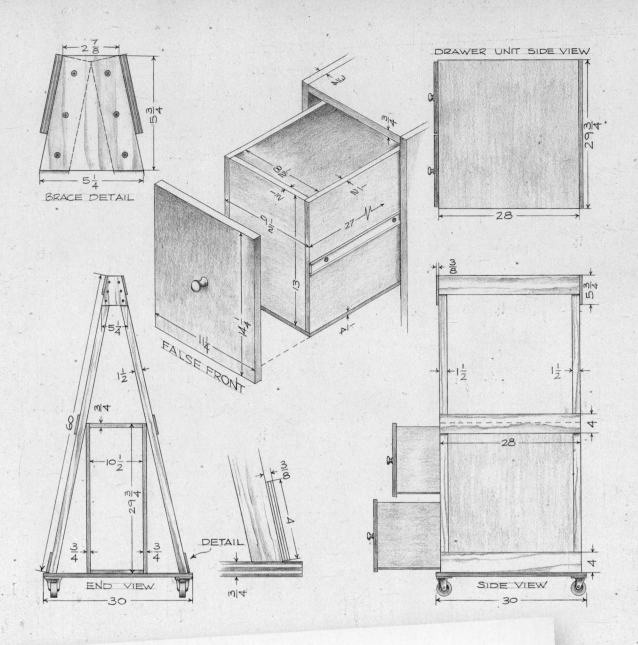

parts list

NO.	COMPONENT	MATERIAL	THICKNESS X WIDTH X LENGTH	
			INCHES	MILLIMETERS
4	A-frame side members	2×2	$1^1/_2 \times 1^1/_2 \times 60$	$38 \times 38 \times 1524$
2	A-frame reinforcing braces	plywood	$^3/_8 \times 5^1/_4 \times 5^3/_4$	$10 \times 133 \times 146$
6	A-frame horizontal braces	plywood	$^3/_8 \times 4 \times 28$	$10 \times 102 \times 711$
1	base	plywood	$^3/_4 \times 30 \times 30$	$19 \times 762 \times 762$
2	drawer unit sides	plywood	$^3/_4 \times 28 \times 29^3/_4$	$19 \times 711 \times 756$
2	drawer unit top & bottom	plywood	$^3/_4 \times 28 \times 10^1/_2$	$19 \times 711 \times 267$
1	drawer unit back	plywood	$^3/_4 \times 12 \times 29^3/_4$	$19 \times 305 \times 756$
2	drawer false front	plywood	$^3/_4 \times 11^1/_4 \times 14^1/_4$	$19 \times 286 \times 362$
2	drawer front & back	plywood	$^1/_2 \times 8^1/_2 \times 13$	$13 \times 216 \times 330$
2	drawer sides	plywood	$^1/_2 \times 13 \times 27$	$13 \times 330 \times 686$
2	drawer bottoms	plywood	$^1/_4 \times 9^1/_2 \times 27$	$6 \times 241 \times 686$
4	3" casters • 2 sets 28" full-extension drawer slides			
2	cabinet door pulls • 4 $1^1/_2$" × $1^1/_2$" metal L-brackets			

❶ The sides of the rack are held together by small reinforcing braces that can be quickly and safely cut out using the band saw.

❷ Using a miter saw, cut the 12° angles on the bottom of each leg of the A-frame side members.

❸ Using glue and screws, attach the reinforcing plates to the A-frame side members. The alignment is correct if the bottom of the triangle measures 28".

❹ The two sides are fastened together with six horizontal braces screwed to the top, middle, and bottom of the sides. In addition to adding stability to the rack as a whole, the middle braces provide support for shorter clamps.

❺ Using screws, attach the casters to the bottom of the base plate.

❻ I attached the rack assembly to the base plate using metal L-brackets. I positioned them on the inside of the rack where they are less visible.

❼ Although I'm not too squeezed for space in my shop, I'm still interested in building really efficient storage solutions, so I decided to construct a cabinet to fit into the interior of the clamp rack. If necessary, it can be removed and used elsewhere in the shop. The cabinet is a five-sided box. Tack the parts together with a nailer and then reinforce all of the joints with screws.

❽ The drawers are easy to make–glue and nails fasten the sides to the fronts and backs and the bottoms are attached using screws. I attached the drawer slides in the cabinet first, set the bottom drawer into place and screwed the slides to the sides of the drawer. I established the height of the top drawer by using a pair of $3/4$"-thick spacers placed on the top of the lower drawer. I used some scrap walnut plywood for the drawer fronts. A pair of simple brass knobs finished off the project.

Modern
END TABLE

AN end table that is different and not too hard to make will match very nicely with the modern furniture of today. Stock used is either walnut or mahogany throughout. The base can be built up in pine and then veneered with a darker wood. The legs are band sawed from 1½-inch stock and taper cut as shown in the detail sketch. These can be tapered on the band saw or on the jointer. The bottom of the legs are rounded on a shaper by using a template as shown in photo in circle. For best results in drilling the holes in the legs for dowels a drill press vise is used as shown in photo below. The top is made from either ½ or 7/16 inch stock, although a heavy plate glass could be substituted. The finish should be made to match the other pieces of furniture or maple wood could be used and finished in natural.

Above photo shows method of shaping the round edges of the legs with a template.

Photo at left shows method of drilling dowel holes on the drill press with a drill press vise.

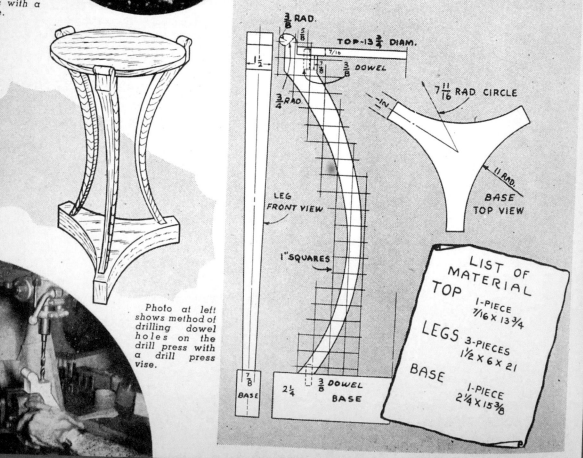

⅜ RAD.
⅝
1½
TOP-13¾ DIAM.
7/16
⅞
⅜ DOWEL
¾ RAD.
7 11/16 RAD. CIRCLE
1N

LEG FRONT VIEW

1" SQUARES

BASE TOP VIEW
11 RAD.

⅞ BASE
2¼
⅜ DOWEL
BASE

LIST OF MATERIAL

TOP
1-PIECE
7/16 X 13¾

LEGS 3-PIECES
1½ X 6 X 21

BASE
1-PIECE
2¼ X 15⅜

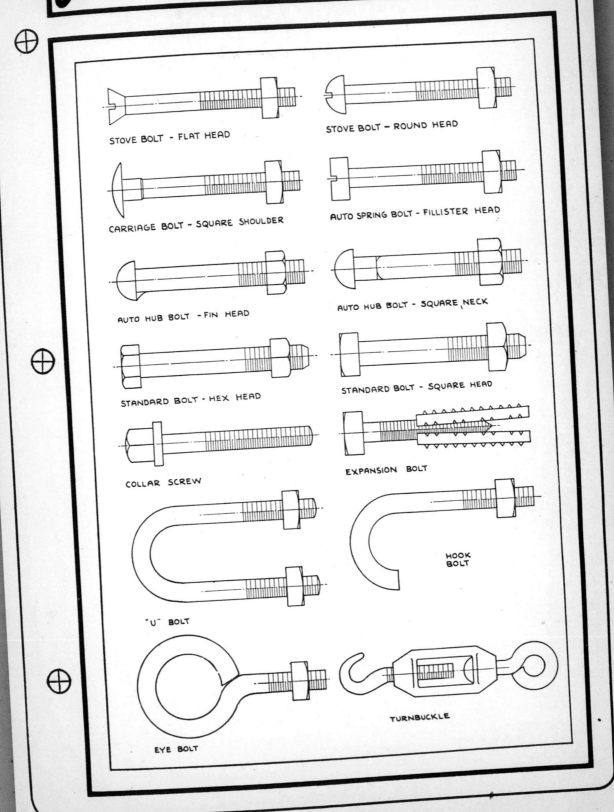

STOVE BOLT – FLAT HEAD

STOVE BOLT – ROUND HEAD

CARRIAGE BOLT – SQUARE SHOULDER

AUTO SPRING BOLT – FILLISTER HEAD

AUTO HUB BOLT – FIN HEAD

AUTO HUB BOLT – SQUARE NECK

STANDARD BOLT – HEX HEAD

STANDARD BOLT – SQUARE HEAD

COLLAR SCREW

EXPANSION BOLT

HOOK BOLT

"U" BOLT

EYE BOLT

TURNBUCKLE

ROLLING WORKSTATION

23

This workstation accomplishes a lot in a small amount of space. I use it to store power tools and accessories, as a sturdy work area for assembling cabinets and furniture and it's easy to wheel around the shop to where it is needed most. It features an integral power strip so I can have a number of tools plugged in at once.

One of my goals for the workstation was to provide outfeed support for my table saw sled. I had planned on routing a set of grooves into the top that would have matched the ones on the table saw's top, but I realized that even with locking casters, it might be tricky to keep the workstation perfectly aligned with the table saw. I solved the problem by designing the workstation to be $1/2"$ lower than the top of the table saw so that the runners on the bottom of my table saw sled could ride across the work surface of the bench.

The size of the workstation is based on my storage needs and the amount of space in my shop. If you build a similar model for yourself, modify it to best suit your own situation. Some other options that make this bench even more useful would be to add drawers, cabinet doors or a flip-up extension for more workspace.

Above, at left, is shown one corner in the shop of Dr. W. H. Lange, Chicago, Ill. Dr. Lange has a complete Delta shop and a fine array of hand tools. Note the cardboard cylinder retained on the drill press—a kink adopted by many drill press users. ● At the top, center, is shown the corner lathe cabinet in the shop of T. E. Conrad, Jersey City, N. J. It takes the usually awkward right angle tool rest quite nicely. ● Top right pictures the shop of Guy E. Blodgett, Marshfield, Wis. While not apparent in this particular picture, Mr. Blodgett has one of the most complete shops on record. Notice the slanting tool panel at the left, and the handy arrangement of corner benches.

In the circle DeQ. Briggs, S are ardent craft this upstairs shop. ● Below Philadelphia, Pa. Mr. Silve portable bench shown at the shop right in his studio. space is at a premium.

J. C. Spooner, Eustis, Florida, solves a vexing problem with a simple stovepipe sawdust chute.

parts list

NO.	COMPONENT	MATERIAL	THICKNESS X WIDTH X LENGTH	
			INCHES	MILLIMETERS
2	sides	MDF	$^3/_4 \times 30^1/_4 \times 42$	$19 \times 768 \times 1067$
1	bottom	MDF	$^3/_4 \times 34^1/_2 \times 42$	$19 \times 876 \times 1067$
1	center divider	MDF	$^3/_4 \times 29^1/_2 \times 34^1/_2$	$19 \times 749 \times 876$
4	fixed shelves	MDF	$^3/_4 \times 20^1/_4 \times 34^1/_2$	$19 \times 514 \times 876$
2	bracing strips	MDF	$^3/_4 \times 4 \times 34^1/_2$	$19 \times 102 \times 876$
1	worksurface	MDF	$^3/_4 \times 44 \times 48$	$19 \times 1118 \times 1219$
4	$2^1/_2$" casters	• 1 power strip		

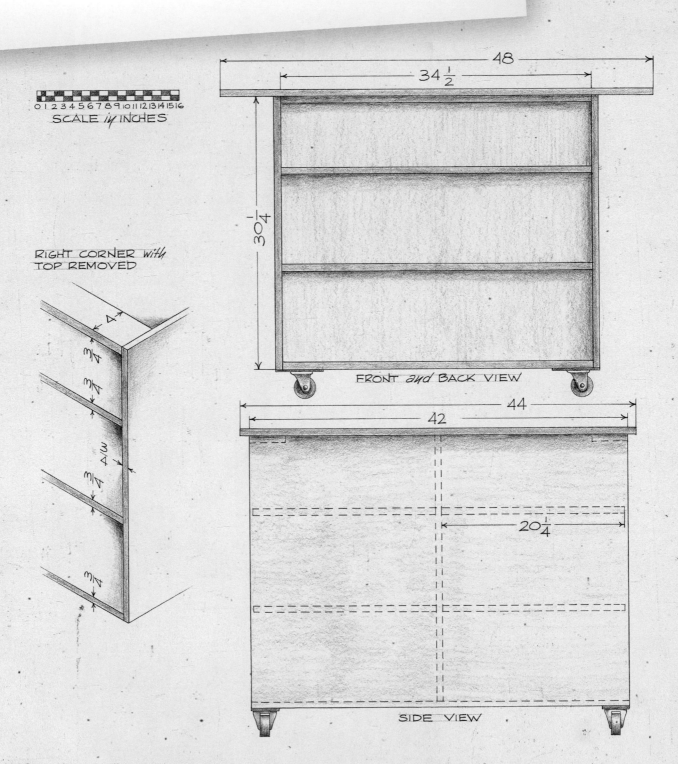

SCALE in INCHES

RIGHT CORNER with TOP REMOVED

FRONT and BACK VIEW

SIDE VIEW

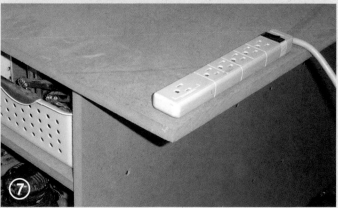

❶ I began by creating a U-shaped component with the sides and bottom. I used glue and countersunk screws to make the assembly.

❷ The assembly gained a great deal of stiffness with the addition of a center panel.

❸ Before the workstation was fully outfitted and took on a lot of weight, I tipped it onto its top and screwed on the casters.

❹ The center panel divided the workstation into two halves. I outfitted both halves of the workstation with fixed shelves. I had considered using adjustable shelves but I knew the objects I'd be storing were all within the same size range, so I used fixed shelves. A pair of 10"-high spacers held the shelves while I screwed them in place.

❺ I attached a pair of bracing strips across the top of the workstation to provide an easy way of securing the worksurface to the cabinet.

❻ The worksurface is screwed to the workstation from below. It can be easily replaced should it ever become damaged.

❼ I screwed a power strip to the top of the unit where it is easily accessible. It could also be attached to one of the side panels.

A CRAFTSMAN BUILDS A HOME

The photographs on this page picture the living room and one of the bedrooms in the "homey" little cottage built by Mr. H. L. Kirsh at Fox Lake, Wisconsin. The house, interior walls and practically all of the furniture was built by Mr. Kirsh in his fully-equipped workshop. That's him at the left, and evidences of work done on his favorite tool can be seen in the wall treatment of the living room interior. (Story on page 87).

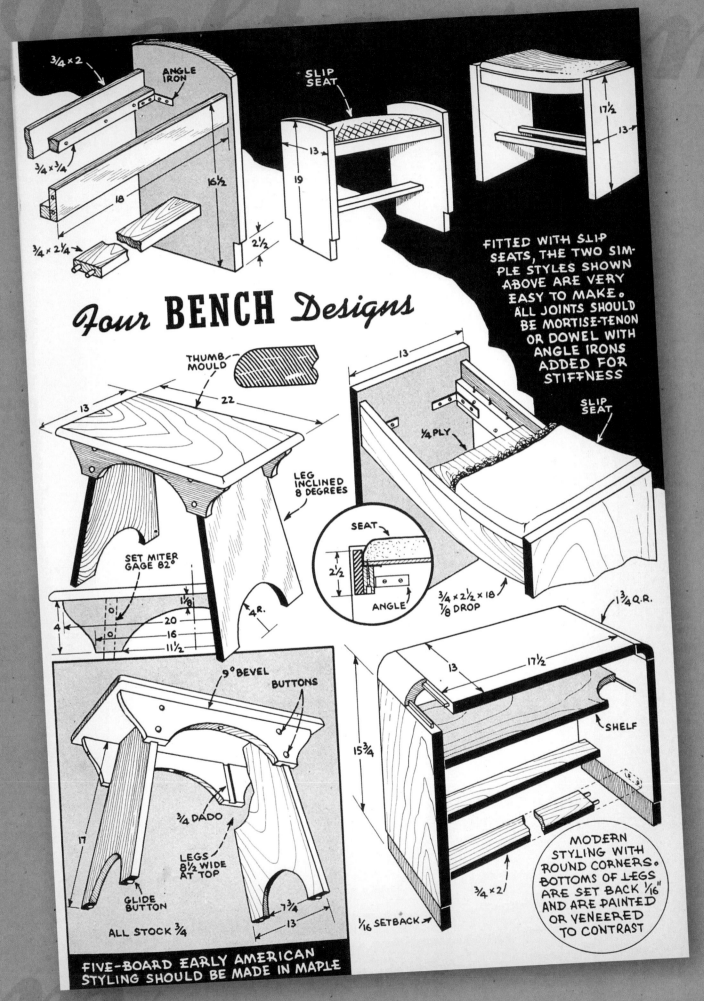

Four BENCH Designs

3/4 × 2
ANGLE IRON
3/4 × 3/4
18
16½
3/4 × 2¼
2½

SLIP SEAT
13
19

SLIP SEAT
17½
13

FITTED WITH SLIP SEATS, THE TWO SIMPLE STYLES SHOWN ABOVE ARE VERY EASY TO MAKE. ALL JOINTS SHOULD BE MORTISE-TENON OR DOWEL WITH ANGLE IRONS ADDED FOR STIFFNESS

THUMB MOULD
13
22
LEG INCLINED 8 DEGREES
SET MITER GAGE 82°
4
1/8
20
16
11½
4 R.

13
¼ PLY
SLIP SEAT

SEAT
2½
ANGLE
3/4 × 2½ × 18
7/8 DROP

1¾ Q.R.
13
17½
15¾
SHELF
3/4 × 2'
1/16 SETBACK

9° BEVEL
BUTTONS
17
3/4 DADO
LEGS 8½ WIDE AT TOP
GLIDE BUTTON
7¾
13
ALL STOCK 3/4

MODERN STYLING WITH ROUND CORNERS. BOTTOMS OF LEGS ARE SET BACK 1/16" AND ARE PAINTED OR VENEERED TO CONTRAST

FIVE-BOARD EARLY AMERICAN STYLING SHOULD BE MADE IN MAPLE

TOOL CADDY

24

My workbench used to be so cluttered up that I could barely use it as I had originally intended. Now that I have this nifty tool caddy, I can actually spread my projects out without worrying about knocking over a glue bottle or a box of screws.

The basic concept is straightforward: I needed a convenient, lightweight cart that could hold the basic accessories that I use most often. The kind of stuff that I got tired of constantly removing from cabinets and putting away, like fasteners, adhesives, and measuring tools. The caddy also has a space for some plastic organizers and it can easily be tucked into a corner or below a bench when you don't need it.

Looking in on DELTA SHOPS

ALWAYS interesting to poke your nose inside a Delta shop, for almost every craftsman has a different idea as to how tools should be arranged, and it's a rare shop, indeed, that does not boast some little kink or variation which is all its own. Figures show that the average shop contains three power machines and two motors. Most shops have an abundance of hand tools. Most shops have inadequate outlets for power. Most shops use glass jars, in some form or other, as containers for small hardware. Most of the shops are in the basement. Most of the shops have a nicely cluttered-up, worked-in appearance. All the shops produce. Beginners and old-timers alike favor the circular saw as a basic unit, with the lathe, band saw and drill press following in close order. How does your own shop compare with these statements and pictures?

...is shown the unusual attic workshop of John ...Paul, Minnesota. Both Mr. and Mrs. Briggs ...s, and many a fine piece has gone forth from ...one corner in the shop of Edwin H. Silverman, ...an is an architect, and has invented the clever ...left in order to accommodate an efficient work- ...e idea could well be used in any shop where

Dennis Johnson, West Depere, Wisconsin, has everything handy in this revolving hardware rack.

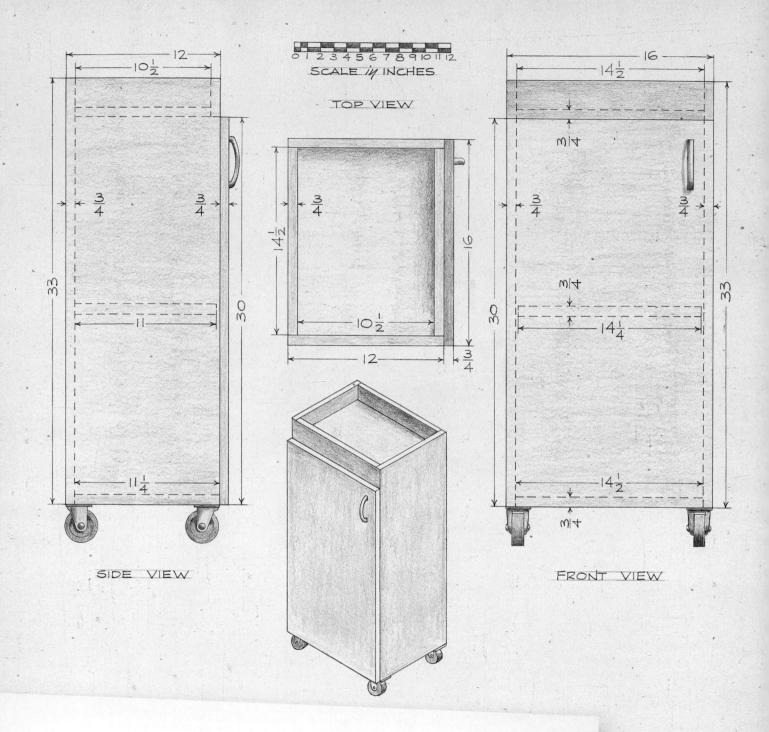

SCALE *in* INCHES

TOP VIEW

SIDE VIEW

FRONT VIEW

parts list

NO.	COMPONENT	MATERIAL	THICKNESS X WIDTH X LENGTH	
			INCHES	MILLIMETERS
2	sides	MDF	¾ × 12 × 33	19 × 305 × 838
1	back	MDF	¼ × 14½ × 33	6 × 368 × 838
1	bottom	MDF	¾ × 11¼ × 14½	19 × 286 × 368
1	shelf	MDF	¾ × 11 × 14¼	19 × 279 × 362
1	front lip	MDF	¾ × 3 × 14½	19 × 76 × 368
1	top	MDF	¾ × 10½ × 14½	19 × 267 × 368
1	door	MDF	¾ × 15¼ × 30	19 × 387 × 838
4	3" castors • 2 European hinges with mounting plates • 1 door pull • 4 shelf pegs			

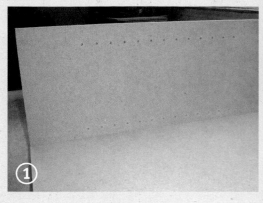

① This organizer only requires a few parts and they can all be cut out using the table saw. The adjustable shelves require holes to be drilled in rows on the interior of the cabinet.

② Screw the back to the sides, then screw the bottoms in place as shown.

③ A key feature of this organizer is the accessible area on top. It has a lip around the edges to keep its contents in place. This is built by nailing the front lip to the top.

④ The sub-assembly, consisting of the top and front lip, is installed using screws.

⑤ The door is hung using European hinges, which require a 35mm ($1^3/8$") hole drilled $1^3/16$" on center from one edge and 4" from each end. Screw the hinges to the door.

⑥ The base plates of the hinges are screwed to the cabinet sides. Then, screw the wheels to the bottom of the cabinet. To avoid splitting the MDF, drill pilot holes first and install the screws.

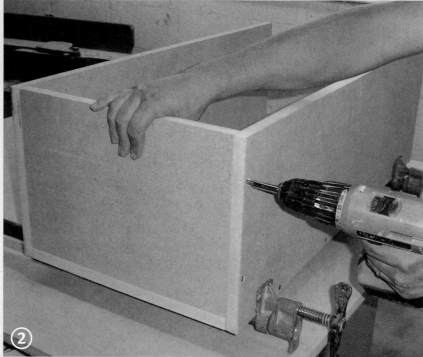

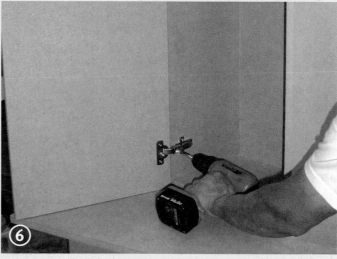

125

SUPPLIERS

**ADAMS & KENNEDY —
THE WOOD SOURCE**
6178 Mitch Owen Rd.
P.O. Box 700
Manotick, ON
Canada K4M 1A6
613-822-6800
www.wood-source.com
Wood supply

ADJUSTABLE CLAMP COMPANY
404 N. Armour St.
Chicago, IL 60622
312-666-0640
www.adjustableclamp.com
Clamps and woodworking tools

B&Q
Portswood House
1 Hampshire Corporate Park
Chandlers Ford
Eastleigh
Hampshire, England SO53 3YX
0845 609 6688
www.diy.com
*Woodworking tools, supplies and
hardware*

BUSY BEE TOOLS
130 Great Gulf Dr.
Concord, ON
Canada L4K 5W1
1-800-461-2879
www.busybeetools.com
Woodworking tools and supplies

**CONSTANTINE'S WOOD CENTER
OF FLORIDA**
1040 E. Oakland Park Blvd.
Fort Lauderdale, FL 33334
800-443-9667
www.constantines.com
Tools, woods, veneers, hardware

**FRANK PAXTON LUMBER
COMPANY**
5701 W. 66th St.
Chicago, IL 60638
800-323-2203
www.paxtonwood.com
Wood, hardware, tools, books

THE HOME DEPOT
2455 Paces Ferry Rd. NW
Atlanta, GA 30339
800-430-3376 (U.S.)
800-628-0525 (Canada)
www.homedepot.com
*Woodworking tools, supplies and
hardware*

KLINGSPOR ABRASIVES INC.
2555 Tate Blvd. SE
Hickory, N.C. 28602
800-645-5555
www.klingspor.com
Sandpaper of all kinds

LEE VALLEY TOOLS LTD.
P.O. Box 1780
Ogdensburg, NY 13669-6780
800-871-8158 (U.S.)
800-267-8767 (Canada)
www.leevalley.com
Woodworking tools and hardware

LOWE'S COMPANIES, INC.
P.O. Box 1111
North Wilkesboro, NC 28656
800-445-6937
www.lowes.com
*Woodworking tools, supplies and
hardware*

MICROPLANE
2401 E. 16th St.
Russellville, AR 72802
800-555-2767
www.us.microplane.com/
*Rotary shaper and other wood-
shaping tools*

**ROCKLER WOODWORKING AND
HARDWARE**
4365 Willow Dr.
Medina, MN 55340
800-279-4441
www.rockler.com
*Woodworking tools, hardware and
books*

TOOL TREND LTD.
140 Snow Blvd. Unit 1
Concord, ON
Canada L4K 4C1
416-663-8665
Woodworking tools and hardware

**TREND MACHINERY & CUTTING
TOOLS LTD.**
Odhams Trading Estate
St. Albans Rd.
Watford
Hertfordshire, U.K.
WD24 7TR
01923 224657
www.trendmachinery.co.uk
Woodworking tools and hardware

VAUGHAN & BUSHNELL MFG. CO.
P. O. Box 390
Hebron, IL 60034
815-648-2446
www.vaughanmfg.com
Hammers and other tools

WATERLOX COATINGS
908 Meech Ave.
Cleveland, OH 44105
800-321-0377
www.waterlox.com
Finishing supplies

WOODCRAFT SUPPLY LLC
1177 Rosemar Rd.
P.O. Box 1686
Parkersburg, WV 26102
800-535-4482
www.woodcraft.com
Woodworking hardware

WOODWORKER'S HARDWARE
P.O. Box 180
Sauk Rapids, MN 56379-0180
800-383-0130
www.wwhardware.com
Woodworking hardware

WOODWORKER'S SUPPLY
1108 N. Glenn Rd.
Casper, WY 82601
800-645-9292
http://woodworker.com
*Woodworking tools and accessories,
finishing supplies, books and plans*

INDEX